"My dear friend and colleague Karynthia Glasper Phillips has paused long enough and often enough to gain this wonderful insight from our wonderful Father God. *Press Pause* is her latest resource that aids those of us who are seeking a unique perspective on growing spiritually. This resource serves to equip and promote our spiritual growth by pausing on purpose and developing productive quiet times and intimacy with the Father God. Her medical training and practical analogies serve not only to enlighten but aid the reader with rewarding applications. So, as Christ invited his disciples to 'come away by yourselves to a secluded place and rest a little while,' I, too, invite you to examine the value of escaping with God in those momentary pauses."

Bishop Horace E. Hockett, founder and overseer of Born Again Church

"In *Press Pause,* Karynthia Glasper Phillips extends an invitation to step away from the noise and rediscover the joy of unhurried time with God. She reminds us that quiet time isn't just another task to check off our to-do list but a lifeline that restores peace, clarity, and strength. What I appreciate most is how she weaves together the practical with deep spiritual insight and biblical wisdom. The included seven-day retreat guide serves as a gentle companion for anyone who longs to be with God, making the practice of daily quiet time not just an ideal to aspire to but a reality to be lived."

Saundra Dalton-Smith, physician-researcher and author of *Sacred Rest*

"Karynthia Glasper Phillips offers a clarion call to pause, pray, and seek God in the midst of life's hurry. With a passion for God, prayer, and the Word, she calls readers to elevate their spiritual appetite beyond the noise of our hurried culture. She addresses the pressing challenges of stress and misplaced priorities, reminding us to pause, breathe, and listen for God's voice. *Press Pause* guides women toward balance, intimacy with God, and fresh faith that calms the soul and elevates the spirit. A must-read for the weary, hungry, and thirsty soul!"

Barbara L. Peacock, founder of Peacock Soul Care Institute and author of *Soul Care in African American Practice, Spiritual Practices for Soul Care,* and *Soul Journey*

"In a world that encourages us to go nonstop, Karynthia Glasper Phillips brings us a gentle reminder to reconnect to the refreshing pauses that enable us to experience the rejuvenation and reset needed to carry the weight of life and ministry effectively."

James McCarroll, author of *PROCEED: A Devotional for Nervous Leaders*

"*Press Pause* prescribes a spiritual strategy for resilience, well-being, and peace in a world where hectic lifestyles define our standard of living. Karynthia Glasper Phillips provides clinical perspective, practical tools, and personal insight to guide readers to remedy the infection of chaos and discover health that is soul deep. I highly recommend this for those seeking an antidote to the busyness epidemic plaguing our modern world."

Tina Yeager, licensed mental health counselor, holistic emotional wellness and purpose coach, and host of the *Flourish Today* radio show and the *Flourish-Meant* podcast

"*Press Pause* is a book written for a time such as this. It's an invitation for every woman who is longing to live with greater intention and divine purpose. Author Karynthia Glasper Phillips offers encouragement in a gentle voice, even as she urges us on to boldness. This book is written with a strong foundation of biblical wisdom for women navigating full lives while seeking deeper intimacy with God. She reminds us God doesn't demand perfection—he calls us to progress, rooted in grace and filled with the Spirit's power. It's a must-read for anyone ready to pursue the 'more' of God in the middle of real life."

Edie Melson, director of the Blue Ridge Mountains Christian Writers Conference

"For women who are exhausted, burned out, and filled with anxiety, Karynthia Glasper Phillips has written a prescription: quiet time. In her book *Press Pause*, she offers a refreshingly practical and spiritually grounded guide to reclaiming daily quiet time with God. Rooted in biblical insight, the book is framed around a devotional journey that helps readers form meaningful habits of stillness, followed by a seven-day retreat to deepen that practice. Phillips thoughtfully connects spiritual intimacy with physical well-being and communal care, offering tools that don't add more to your schedule but weave sacred pauses into everyday life. *Press Pause* is an encouraging invitation to pause, reflect, and encounter God amid the chaos."

Janet Holm McHenry, inspirational speaker and author of *PrayerWalk* and *Praying Personalities*

"This is an awesome book that equips you with the skills and practical approaches to cultivate and develop your personal relationship with our heavenly Father. *Press Pause* is an informative resource that gently reminds us as believers to make it our business to carve out alone time with God for true refreshment, because he is the source and the answer to all our needs."

Sydney Ann Johnson, author of *God, The Great I AM*

"*Press Pause* is a call for busy women everywhere to recognize the need for quiet time. Karynthia Glasper Phillips encourages women who are juggling life, motherhood, and more to lean into God's presence. Spending time with our Creator should not be an afterthought but our first thought every day!"

Victoria Riollano, psychology professor and author of *Warrior Mother*

PRESS
PAUSE

*Making Time for God
in an Overscheduled Life*

Karynthia Glasper Phillips

Foreword by CeCe Winans

ivp

An imprint of InterVarsity Press
Downers Grove, Illinois

InterVarsity Press
P.O. Box 1400 | Downers Grove, IL 60515-1426
ivpress.com | email@ivpress.com

InterVarsity Press® is the publishing division of InterVarsity Christian Fellowship/USA®. For more information, visit intervarsity.org.

All Scripture quotations, unless otherwise indicated, are taken from The Holy Bible, New International Version®, NIV®. Copyright © 1973, 1978, 1984, 2011 by Biblica, Inc.™ Used by permission of Zondervan. All rights reserved worldwide. www.zondervan.com. The "NIV" and "New International Version" are trademarks registered in the United States Patent and Trademark Office by Biblica, Inc.™

Published in association with the Books & Such Literary Management, www.booksandsuch.com.

While any stories in this book are true, some names and identifying information may have been changed to protect the privacy of individuals.

The publisher cannot verify the accuracy or functionality of website URLs used in this book beyond the date of publication.

Cover design: Faceout Studio, Addie Lutzo
Interior design: Jeanna Wiggins
Image: © Pobytov / DigitalVision Vectors via Getty Images

ISBN 978-1-5140-1160-7 (print) | ISBN 978-1-5140-1161-4 (digital)

Printed in the United States of America ♾

Library of Congress Cataloging-in-Publication Data
Names: Phillips, Karynthia Glasper, 1961- author
Title: Press pause : making time for God in an overscheduled life /
   Karynthia Glasper Phillips.
Description: Downers Grove, IL : IVP, [2026] | Includes bibliographical
   references.
Identifiers: LCCN 2025039374 (print) | LCCN 2025039375 (ebook) | ISBN
   9781514011607 paperback | ISBN 9781514011614 ebook
Subjects: LCSH: Christian women–Prayers and devotions | Christian
   women–Religious life | Spiritual retreats for women
Classification: LCC BV4844 .P49 2026 (print) | LCC BV4844 (ebook)
LC record available at https://lccn.loc.gov/2025039374
LC ebook record available at https://lccn.loc.gov/2025039375

31   30   29   28   27   26 | 8   7   6   5   4   3   2   1

I dedicate this book to

my mother, mentor, and friend,

Virginia Hazel Armstrong Glasper.

Mom, you taught me the power of fellowship

with God and humanity. Your legacy continues to

ignite my passion for quiet times that spark revival

in prayer, Scripture reading, and worship

for victorious daily living for his glory.

CONTENTS

FOREWORD

CeCe Winans

A s a gospel singer and songwriter who desires to draw people into closer connections with God, I know the importance of making room for God in our daily schedules, and I pray readers will use this treasure to help them do just that.

Many women's overscheduled lives make adding anything to the daily routine, including quiet time with God, feel like a burdensome, heavy load. Finding time, even a few precious moments to spend in solitude, seems an unattainable goal. The result? God gets pushed to the outer edges of many women's lives. Lacking the wisdom of God gleaned through close fellowship with him, they then unnecessarily contend with public and private issues. Many women struggle with the question of how to create space for God in an overscheduled life.

Press Pause answers this question by providing a comprehensive toolkit rooted in Bible reading, prayer, reflective journaling, and recitation of Scripture. Karynthia Glasper Phillips reminds us that no one is immune to the pressures of life that work to dilute faith, obedience, and spiritual connection. But she offers hope through this dynamic resource designed to help Christians reset their spiritual lives at any time during the year. It gently guides readers on a self-discovery tour of their relationship with God and on to a sturdy path of consistent relationship building. It offers a path to spiritual redirection, especially for women grappling with spiritual disconnection. Its gentle mentoring tone is free from condemnation, making it a great resource for Christian women of all ages, regardless of how long they've been walking with God.

Drawing from her decades of experience as a medical professional and ordained minister, Karynthia offers unique insight into achieving a healthy balance of physical and spiritual wholeness. With refreshing honesty and transparency about her spiritual journey and her physical challenges—including a bout with cancer—she shares personal stories to unmask the façade of self-sufficiency. Those relatable personal experiences help readers know they are not alone in the struggle to grow spiritually.

Each chapter concludes with a reflection and prayer. An exciting feature is the seven-day personal retreat offering a plan for consistently spending a week drawing closer to God. It's a unique aspect of the book that encourages you to immediately put into practice everything that you've learned about the importance of spending quality alone time with God. If you've been asking for a sign as to whether it's time to get alone with God, *Press Pause* is it.

Most of us know that getting back on track spiritually can be difficult without guided help. That's why *Press Pause* is needed today. Don't rush through the pages. *Press Pause* is designed to help you beat that urge to rush through life mindlessly doing everything on your to-do list except slow down for time with God. So press pause on your activities and commit to applying what you read so you can flourish spiritually. By doing so, you'll ensure that you can "pause on purpose" on a more consistent basis while enjoying life abundantly, both naturally and spiritually.

I have known Karynthia Glasper Phillips for many years, and she has been a blessing in my life! Her love for God and his people has been consistent through the years. I know that what God has given her in this book to share with the world will bring forth godly fruit in the lives of all those who read it, for his glory!

Introduction

A CALL TO SPIRITUAL MATURITY

THIS BOOK IS FOR WOMEN of all ages who want to be infused with God's power, women who are juggling to balance personal and professional life but want more of God. Women in various fields often balance multiple roles—stay-at-home mom, ministry leader, or full-time career person—and may face challenges in integrating spirituality into their daily lives. This book is written for those who desire more of God while pursuing their God-given purpose.

God gave us tools for communicating with him that we can use anytime: The issue is when and how. We don't have to wait to enter a building designed for worship. Communicating with God is free and only requires our undivided attention and finding time in our over-scheduled lives. We need only pause long enough to build a trusting relationship with God our Father. This occurs as we honor time scheduled to meet him. In this book, we unpack the value and purpose of private moments of prayer, praise, worship, and reflective journaling. We will find this book as an instrument to appreciate the presence of God, as it stimulates us to enter the sacredness of rest. Together we will "slow our roll" and pause to discern what God says about our unique purpose and contributions to the kingdom and the world.

No matter your level of spiritual maturity, join us as we dive deeper into finding the treasure of his presence to keep us oriented toward our calling throughout the hustle and bustle of the day.

There are times when regular congregational worship and other spiritual activities fall into a routine. For example, we may be familiar with some congregation members' habits of worship, who regularly cry, dance, or shout during a church service. We are all at different stages in our relationship with God in public, and he knows how sincere we are in our various worship expressions. Corporate worship plays a significant role in spiritual development, but private time is equally essential for achieving spiritual maturity.

Salvation is personal, so it stands to reason that we should understand the requirement to learn about God on an individual basis. Secret times spent with God shouldn't be a routine check-off item but a true drenching of the spirit and soul. After all the hype, shouting, and socializing in the church building or in small group settings, what happens when we are alone? How do we communicate with God? How often do we embrace his presence? What happens when we need an answer, healing, or direction in a spiritual battle? Knowing God personally helps us develop confidence in our spiritual connection to trust his Word as we are obedient.

This book invites you to seek and experience spiritual growth and direction from God in private times of saturation in the presence of the Holy Spirit. We will move together in solitude from spiritual poverty or a lukewarm spirit to a rich abundance of faith and grace to live a life of victory. In your overscheduled life, find keys to peaceful success—they will unfold as you pace yourself in created spaces in your schedule. Taking time is not only necessary for public spiritual fellowship, but also for private relational development with God. When we separate from the rush of life, we learn the significance of being children of God. In private moments, we remember that God's power helps us live freed from worldly influences and find rest in knowing he is well able to do above what we ask in prayer.

This book can be used for small groups, congregational Bible study, personal Bible study, or as a resource for spiritual/discipleship. Weekly church worship services, Sunday school, midweek Bible study, Friday night fellowship, and other activities are excellent aids in developing spiritual maturity; however, learning to engage with God personally allows an experience with him on a whole new level. By pausing on purpose and abiding in God's presence, his peace refreshes and enhances our daily routines and allows favorable outcomes through various circumstances that try to interrupt our to-do list.

You will be guided through three sections. Part one provides a biblical foundation for why intimate morning moments to honor God are vital to Christian living. The terms *pause on purpose*, *POP*, *press pause*, *just pause*, and *quiet time* or *pivot* are used interchangeably to express the idea of slowing down long enough for intentional times alone with God. These moments, or times of sabbath rest, in God's presence help recalibrate spiritual imbalances, impacting the functionality of mind and body over time. The act of pivoting during your day allows your thoughts to relinquish distractions and hear the voice of God for encouragement, or to make a necessary decision in your life.

The backstory of this book is about how I discovered quiet time as a remedy bringing wholeness during my recovery as a fragmented woman who'd become trapped in the maze of busyness. A pause is necessary for all women to survive the race to purpose, no matter the cost, to reorient their focus on well-being. Brokenness often exists without women realizing it; they are deaf to the call of the Holy Spirit, and the body's signal of imbalance—failure to respond in pause and reset—leads to many women's spiritual, emotional, and physical detriment. At the beginning of this introduction, I mentioned that God provides tools to communicate with him through a pause during quiet times, but let's dive deeper into why. He desires us to be whole. It begins with returning to the basics, to dedicating devotional time to appreciate how intricately he has made us.

The tools he provides are extensions of his compassion for us with the goal of spending eternal life with him. They are tools to empower us to live whole (balanced) lives on earth with joy. It is during the pause that you will recognize these tools: one fixes imbalances, and the other sustains us during chronic stress loads before an exhaustive breakdown occurs. This is accomplished by homeostasis and allostatic load. Both are mechanisms that aid in our bodies' ability to maintain

equilibrium, but they help in different ways. Indeed, they are physiological terms that have spiritual implications for our well-being:

1. Homeostasis repairs imbalances in the body to restore
   equilibrium.
2. Allostatic load sustains the body's equilibrium under accumu-
   lated stress.

Both mechanisms can become impaired, adversely affecting the
body with disease, emotional instability, and may end in death. Spiritually, when we put off time in prayer and listening for God in both
spiritual and natural matters, the weight of life can wear us thin,
triggering illnesses such as hypertension, rheumatoid arthritis,
chronic fatigue syndrome, depression . . . you name it. Your slowing
down in moments of pause is the catalyst for a better you. Keep these
two terms in your mind, or jot in your journal to ponder which provision is most operative in your overscheduled life.

Part one is also designed to help you evaluate your spiritual appetite
to determine whether your spiritual palate craves the things of God,
or if you have adopted a taste for items that compromise your spiritual
growth and development. It will help you assess whether you are
healthy, spiritually hungry, or starving. It can be used to explore your
current relationship status with the Father.

God has provided a mechanism—the Holy Spirit—that works like
homeostasis does naturally in the human body. Physical *homeostasis*
refers to "any process that living things use to actively maintain fairly
stable conditions necessary for survival."[1] When something is out of
whack, the body's systems will recognize the change and work to
regain homeostasis to protect physical health. Similarly, our spirits
seek to maintain spiritual homeostasis, like a global positioning system
(GPS) that provides guidance and location correction for a particular
destination. The Holy Spirit acts like a sensor, alerting us to spiritual
disconnections. We can heed the alerts and make corrective actions
that can prevent forms of destruction.

The good news is that you can circumvent spiritual sickness with full restoration by implementing the strategies in this book. As you progress from chapter to chapter, you will find a devotional at the end of each chapter to serve as a primer to the bonus seven-day retreat in part three of the book. These are called *pause on purpose*, or *POP*, devotionals.

Part two prompts you to remember God's love for you, no matter the state of your spiritual condition. Regardless of your relationship with God, your Christian walk will be strengthened by encouraging purposeful pauses and brief quiet moments. Part two will renew your faith, build hope, help you find peace, and position you to receive favor from God and man to live as a champion.

Part three will guide you through a seven-day retreat with daily activities aimed at enhancing your implementation of moments of pause in the presence of the Holy Spirit. This devotional journey includes tools for spiritual development toward maturity with self-discovery assessments, prayer guides, and Scriptures for meditation and memorization. Each day of the journey includes action items that provide practical application of the concepts related to pausing on purpose. I recommend using a journal to record your responses, as this will enliven your experience during the seven-day journey. Include thoughts about devotional readings, Scriptures being studied, revelations from the Lord while in quiet meditation, and what you experience in personal worship. These notes and journal entries can be reviewed throughout the day or later, providing more complete insight into what God spoke to you personally, and serve as a reminder of guidance received from the Holy Spirit.

If you are reading this book, you are ready for a change. Pausing to prioritize God is hard work, but you have made the first step. Bible teacher Elizabeth George says, "Beginning each day with God will change your priorities."[2] Decide when, where, and what time you will meet God every day. Early morning is good for setting the tone and aligning your daily schedules and tasks with God's will. In preparation for personal time with God, I place my small tote bag with a book, my Bible, pen, and journal in the great room near my sitting chair. I play music softly as I enter worship and become still to begin my reading. It is important to use your Bible, not your phone or tablet, for reading. Consider putting away devices and applications, to eliminate notifications and the temptation to scroll through social media. It is fine to use a device for music only. Sisters, spot a comfy chair and a glass of water, and keep reading for spiritual transformation that impacts the health of your spirit, mind, and body.

POIA

In the process of spiritual development, I follow these four steps when reading the Bible. You can use them to engage with Scripture for additional understanding and relevance as you read each chapter.

1. Posture of prayer: Read and pray in a comfortable place to hear God's voice.
2. Observation: What is being said? What is going on? What is the context? Paraphrase or put your name in the passage.
3. Interpretation: What is it saying? What does it mean to you? Is it relevant? Do you perceive spiritual meaning?
4. Application: How can you apply this lesson today? What is your plan of obedience to the Scripture?

POIA is a clarifying tool for Scripture dissection. It allows you to center yourself, investigate, discern, and listen to how the Scriptures are guiding you and how you will respond to his voice. My prayer is that you give yourself grace as you read and practice pause. Allow the Holy Spirit to awaken you morning by morning. He will heighten the sensitivity of your ears to hear, learn, and help you apply what he teaches you in the quietness of pause (Isaiah 50:4-5). By slowing down to read the Bible, you are becoming spiritually healthy with wisdom to take better care of yourself.[3] This leads to consistent spiritual homeostasis as women fashioned in his image, with strategies to minimize anxiety and acquire peace, while increasing productivity in the home, workplace, ministry, and other settings. Finding time for God in an overscheduled life assures victorious living.

MY PRAYER FOR YOU

Father, give each woman who reads this book the strength to move through these pages with hope and renewed freedom to pause from the world's system of motion for success. Help them to seek first the kingdom of God wholeheartedly and trust you to work behind the scenes, managing those things that concern them as they spend time with you. We partner with you to become better equipped to serve and lead others, as we enjoy the abundance of guilt-free self-care for a healthier, totally fit woman.

Part 1

BALANCE THE JUGGLING ACT

Things on the floor can wait.

LILIANA KOHANN

1

GOD, I NEED YOUR HELP

*The LORD replied, "My Presence will go with you,
and I will give you rest."*

EXODUS 33:14

SISTERS, ARE YOU "RUNNING ON FUMES" AND feeling broken, fragmented, overwhelmed, or uninspired? Perhaps you may be experiencing all this at the same time. Women, in general, are in a web of entanglement to survive in varied pursuits, such as climbing the ladder in corporate America, serving in church leadership, or engaging in community activism, in addition to personal and family responsibilities. Women of all racial and ethnic backgrounds are challenged to endure the duality of gender and economic suppression. In addition, Black, Indigenous, and other women of color (BIWOC) carry triple burdens in light of racism, sexism, and limited opportunities for economic advancement. How do you stay on top of your game with so many challenges and obstacles? Who or what is your stabilizing force?

Because there is a constant act of juggling multiple roles at different life stages and seasons, it is absolutely necessary for women to find time and space to experience God's presence. The frequency of reset for balanced living is necessary for the well-being of our spirit, mind, and body. Together let us press pause in an act of surrender, making a conscious choice to decline less important things competing for our attention and intentionally sit at the feet of God. The posture of surrender is the bending of our ear to the heart of God to listen to his will for our lives. A purpose-driven pause on the speedway of daily existence helps us obtain and maintain spiritual health for balanced living. Lasting productivity begins when we regularly stop and enter his presence—a zone of renewed strength, focus, peace, and enlightenment.

The fragility of a woman is impacted most when her spirit, soul, and body are disjointed, and internal homeostasis is in crisis—a weak spirit sickens the soul. Wholeness begins with understanding how to maintain spiritual homeostasis, the core plank of humanity's functionality. Why? When one is spiritually healthy, the entire physical body benefits. The three parts of the human body are spirit, mind, and body. Each component requires attention; however, this book focuses on spiritual health, the core of the trifold being. A healthy, stable spirit fortifies unity (harmony) of all parts of our being (spirit, soul, and body).

Come away, beloved, to a nonjudgmental space with the Holy Spirit to gain access into the private chamber where hearts meet with a loving and forgiving God. In the journey through these pages, you will encounter transformation in the presence of God. You will learn to slow down and press pause in the privacy of your own space or a small group. The challenge is to remain still long enough in God's presence to discern God's character in Scripture, prayer, reflection, and journaling, building renewed faith to trust him as you navigate life. This book is a companion that will enhance the process of pressing pause from nonessential tasks that fill your calendar, robbing time from God, leaving your spirit empty. In this contemporary contemplative experience, you will discover how to find solitude, engage attentively, and listen to God constantly in steering your spiritual journey. As author John Mark Comer says, "Hurry kills relationships. Love takes time; hurry doesn't have it. It kills joy, gratitude, and appreciation; people in a rush don't have time to enter the goodness of the moment. It kills wisdom; wisdom is born in the quiet, the slow."[1]

TIME CULTIVATES TRUST

Relationship building with God takes time. Think about how much time people spend with their boyfriend or girlfriend before saying "I do." My friend and husband, Tim, and I spent many days and nights on the phone because we wanted to be together and know everything about each other. Friendship builds trust and confidence in one another. A spiritually healthy relationship with God the Father also involves time to build trust in his counsel and promises.

It is easy to go to God in difficult situations such as financial needs, rebellious children, and sickness. He wants us to come to him when we recognize we need him, but why wait until we have an emergency or are in crisis, crying or completely losing our composure? Why do we not cry out to him when we are happy, grateful, and thankful for his blessings? Practicing pause builds confidence to talk to God anytime, regardless of the situation, embracing his kindness and comforting guidance. Here's the real test of obedience: Will we pause and choose an unconditional love and purpose-driven relationship with him?

My grandmother, at ninety-one, is a perfect example of a life committed to a relationship with God. Early one morning, she was awakened, got out of bed, and knelt to pray while breakfast was being prepared. When she did not come in to eat, her daughter looked in on her and realized that her mother had transitioned to heaven while in that posture of prayer. While sad for her loved ones, it was a beautiful sight to remember. When we got the call and my mother told us that Grandma died, it did not feel sad to me. I felt like she was honored to be called home while in communication with God. There was no sense of fear about her death; my grandmother's friendship and relationship with God removed any fear, guilt, and doubt because I knew she loved God and he loved her—they were in covenant.

He is our Father and friend, so he should never be approached in fear of harm, but in reverence, yielding to his Spirit and hearing his whispers of love. You can be free to trust and not doubt, having no guilt or shame. There are times we will fail, but we have Jesus, our

Advocate with the Father God, and can sincerely apologize, be forgiven, and forgive ourselves even when we are missing our time with him.

PRIORITIZE GOD OVER OUR CULTURE OF STRESS

Would you agree that women have gravitated toward God more than men throughout the ages? They have wholeheartedly served the church, organizations, employers, and families. Each of these relationships requires sacrifices of time, often to the point of self-neglect. It is not easy to properly balance it all, but it can be done when daily goals are set to prioritize relationship with the Father. Making time for God guarantees productive days yielding fruit that will remain.

The world is moving at a faster and faster pace. Thanks to modern technology, we are always plugged in to our jobs, distressing news reports, and what our friends, family, and favorite celebrities share on social media. Modern advances were meant to make our lives easier and more interconnected, yet they often leave us anxious and overwhelmed. We are fearful of not doing or being enough. In other words, we have developed *FOMO*—the fear of missing out—which is now so prevalent that the term has made its way into the *Oxford English Dictionary*.

As a longtime medical professional, I have observed that stressful lifestyles without intervals of pause to reset contribute to various health problems. Few know how to get a real handle on their out-of-control lives. They seek answers for success and peace by self-medicating and through other indulgences, far too often falling into sin and other traps of the enemy. The solution for regaining peace and productivity is found in the simple choice of pause, an old practice of contemplation.

Hurry has become the driving force of humanity, minimizing or eliminating time with the One who has the blueprint for every individual's purpose in life. The not-so-distant Covid-19 pandemic opened the eyes of many to the need to pause and reset from life in the fast lane. Many have returned to past behavior patterns, however, in attempts to redeem time and offset the loss of material gain because of the pandemic.

Ladies, we are in a pandemic that has existed for ages—bearers-of-life loads. Whether you are a pastor's wife, preacher, teacher, speaker, business owner, doctor, lawyer, or homemaker, societal pressure can stack up, hindering the practice of pause, excluding the practice of God's guidance for obedience and self-awareness to eliminate stressors that wear us down into broken pieces. This is not a science course, but understanding the necessity of a pause for spiritual and physical reset is vital for women. As you sit at his feet in pause, how has the Spirit been leading you to care for the total you? Are you teetering under the weight of chronic stress?

EXPLORING SPIRITUAL HEALTH

A desire to experience other models of spiritual intimacy led me on an expedition of private and public religious practices. My search began with reading, watching YouTube, and attending conferences. During this immersion, I visited many different types of worship services and temples, and interviewed leaders about their daily practices to nurture spiritual health. The one thing that was consistent among the groups were the influences of time constraints and cultural expectations to perform. The observations revealed that private times of worship seemed to be an optional task. The acts of contemplation required setting boundaries of separateness in solitude to maintain a rhythm of prayer, reading, and reflection—personal time honoring religious covenants. The public groups of worship had designated times of attendance that had some similarity to Western Christian services.

To understand cyclic consistency in spiritual health, I was given the opportunity to experience two monasteries, one in Conception, Missouri, and the other in Thailand. Interestingly enough, the visible culture and practices of prayer and work life in the Missouri monastery remained relatively intact, with little of the fingerprints of outside culture on their tradition. There was little deviation from regular patterns in the Conception community, including prayer twenty-four hours per day, sunlight, rest, and healthy meals. The overall pace of life was slower than in Thailand, which appeared to be more commercial.

In Thailand, the influence of Western culture was evident in the urban areas I visited. For example, there was "table talk" storytelling by the monks in a specific city location, with an ATM nearby for listeners to access and directly pay them for their services. The noise and movement of people were like that of large American cities; it was interesting to watch a monk go and use an ATM like any other person. Closer to the main worship building it became less noisy, but movement and talking were still heard while people located to areas in the temple to pray, worship, and reflect. However, there were other areas and communities that were less accessible to tourists and outsiders that maintained more of their traditional culture of communion in silence.

In that different country and culture, it took serious effort to get into a pause space. In both settings, the goal was to honor religious traditions by making purposeful choices to maintain spiritually healthy relationships—however, in Thailand, it appeared that concessions to outside culture were more necessary for financial reasons.

In a nutshell, a life of peace and success is available, based on the conscious decision and practice of gathering ourselves in quiet to commune with the Father. There is value in slowing down long enough to arouse our consciousness to the presence of God in every situation and circumstance. In the twenty-first century, it seems that contemplation is an overlooked or forgotten spiritual practice. This neglect may very well be a contributing factor to the increase of immoral lifestyles, as many lack "God-consciousness" or awareness of his love, character, grace, and mercy amid sinful disobedience and a life of busyness.

In the following pages, I pray that you chart a course for this journey; pause on purpose as necessary; learn to minimize and eliminate needless rushing, hurrying, and worrying from your life; and position yourself in a posture of stillness when needed to limit distractions and stress. This will help maintain focus while increasing discernment, critical-thinking abilities, and overall mental capacity.

It has been my experience that slowing down harnesses the true essence of God's presence. In every situation, we can find a peaceful balance that honors covenant relationships and enhances productivity and fruitfulness in our lifestyles. It is my hope as you continue reading through the chapters and devotionals that practicing moments of pause will lead to daily private and public victorious living.

ARE YOU AT A CROSSROADS?

In the book of Jeremiah, the Lord said, "You are standing at the *crossroads*. So, consider your path. Ask where the old, reliable paths are. Ask where the path is that leads to blessing and follow it. If you do, you will find rest for your souls." But they said, "We will not follow it!" (Jeremiah 6:16 NET, emphasis added). Today our rejection of his way can be demonstrated in our choices to do other things as opposed to following the path that leads to sitting at his feet in times of quiet refreshing.

Many people in our society are at a crossroads, searching for answers to achieve success and finding forms of peace. Popular in the search are self-help books, including parenting, personal renewal, developing interpersonal skills, and spiritual growth. The Bible addresses those topics; however, there is a decline in Bible readers. Research by Lifeway reports that "in January 2023, around 100 million adults, or 39 percent of Americans, said they use the Bible three or more times a year. That equals the lowest number in the 13-year history of the study and ties with last year as the lowest percentage. In 2021, at the height of the pandemic, 128 million Americans (50 percent) said they interacted with Scripture at least that much."[2]

Our world is in a moral crisis: the argument can be made that it is because of diminished quality time with God—including reading the Bible.

There are benefits in reading the Bible. For example, it helps people to be morally and spiritually healthy as they become more aware of God's presence and attuned to the necessity of self-care of the spirit, mind, and body. The research also indicates that those who are engaged in Scripture reading are more *hopeful*.[3]

Other important research supports how Bible engagement substantially and positively impacts our spiritual, emotional, and physical health. As author Kathleen Cooke noted in a 2017 article, the Center for Bible Engagement documented that "if a person engages in the Bible four or more times a week, their odds of drinking in excess fell 62 percent; pornography viewing and sex outside of marriage fell 59 percent; gambling decreased 45 percent; gossiping and lying, 28 percent; and that overeating and mishandling money both fell by 20 percent. Bible engagement also produces more peace and joy in a person's life, by reducing the frequency of various emotional struggles."[4]

As this research continues to show, spending time with God in his Word brings positive change in a person's life. The results of time with God in prayer and Bible reading reveal solutions and an increase in one's quality of life. The Bible tells us in Psalm 119:105, "Your word is a lamp for my feet, a light on my path." Just as he did in the Garden of Eden, God wants to fellowship with us each day. He wants to guide us toward greater peace and purpose, perhaps even reordering our priorities in the process.

God gave us the tools for communicating with him, and we can use them every day. They are free (except for the price of a Bible) and only require a portion of our time. Within the following pages, you will discover the benefits of quiet time—including Bible reading, prayer, praise and worship, and reflective journaling—to help you develop an intimate relationship with God, find answers, and gain practical skills for living your best life. The benefits of quiet time during daily life as well as during life crises become readily apparent as you begin working on your relationship with God.

Now take a deep breath and in the margins of this book describe your current relationship with God in two or three words.

REALITY CHECK

You might think you are too busy for quiet time, but the truth is, you're too busy *not* to find time to spend with God each day. Jesus was fully God while he walked the earth, but he was also fully human. He got tired and had to juggle multiple tasks, just as we do. He, too, had to carve out time to rest and pray. Those times of intimacy empowered him to fulfill his Father's will. We read in Mark 6:31, "Then, because so many people were coming and going that they did not even have a chance to eat, he said to them, 'Come with me by yourselves to a quiet place and get some rest.'" If Jesus took the time to pause on purpose to rest and pray, so must we.

Starting today, you can breathe new life into your relationship with God. Whether you are a new convert or have been a Christian for years, you can grow your relationship with God by spending regular time in his presence. Devoting time to God brings victory in your life. This is the primary reason Satan attempts to distract Christians from consistently spending time with God. He knows the more you learn to trust and depend on God, the less effective his efforts to hinder your destiny will be.

I pray this book refreshes your faith and shows you how to become disciplined in worshiping God, as well as in reading, memorizing, and meditating on the Scriptures. Engaging in worship will invoke the presence of the Holy Spirit to fill you afresh and ignite a yearning to fulfill the call on your life. Studying his Word will equip you to complete the work God has given you to do. Regardless of your career choice, we are all called to intimacy with God. You can have rest, peace, and clear direction for your hectic life by making time for God a daily practice. God created you to fellowship with him, and in that time of fellowship, he will guide you to synchronize your life physically, emotionally, and spiritually.

▌▌ PAUSE ON PURPOSE 1

LORD, HERE I AM

God is faithful, who has called you into fellowship with
his Son, Jesus Christ our Lord. – 1 CORINTHIANS 1:9

Lord, here I am. Sitting at work in the cafeteria, thinking about my missed appointments with you. The song sung by gospel artist Smokie Norful, "I Need You Now," often plays in my head, because it expresses the desperation in my heart to be rescued by God from the demands of chaos. Finding time to meet with God is not difficult compared to societal pressures to perform. God doesn't push us but waits patiently for us to come sit with him. So often I feel like I am compromising in not making accommodation in my schedule for God, often having days with no adequate time with God. Am I attempting to serve two masters? Reverencing my responsibilities of work and church volunteering and ministry more than routine quality time with him?

Acknowledging in prayer that this has been my path by choice, to journey through life many times without you, I am sorry. I have missed you and still love you. Watching the clock on the wall, others rushing to get a bite to eat, worrying about today's deadlines—my soul desires a touch from you. My heart longs for you. I need you now. Knowing you want time with me as my Creator is a delight. My concern is not your faithfulness, but rather my faithfulness to show up. Thank you for your patience, love, and forgiveness. Today, I surrender my will to answer your call to fellowship. My heart cries, "Here I am, Lord."

Friend, where are you on the road of spirituality? God is waiting for you to grant you more.

Do you feel like you are serving two masters? Do you love one more than the other? Why?

The goodness of Jesus is available to you. However, you must do the work of seeking and finding private time with God. No one else can do it for you. When I think of activating progress, I think about some species of turtles; they can't move unless they stick their necks out. Today you stuck your neck out and began an uninterrupted time in prayer, reflection, and Scripture reading. The transforming power of the Holy Spirit is always near, waiting on you.

Reflection: Spiritual reset comes easier when we prioritize regular moments of stillness with God.

Prayer: It's me, Lord, needing you more each day. With my eyes on you, I lift my hands to touch the hem of your Spirit. As you resolve issues and concerns in my life, help me to continue showing up. Thank you for being near.

2

MOVE BEYOND
MISALIGNMENT

THOSE WHO SPEND REGULAR TIME in God's presence successfully carry out God's purpose for their lives. This does not remove all
troubles from their lives, but it causes them to know the assuring
comfort of God's presence during those difficult times.

When you start meeting with God daily, it may feel predictable at
first. But as you begin to experience refreshing peace and joy and see
him working in your life, you will want to linger in God's presence
longer. As you praise, worship, and enjoy fellowship with God, you
notice him giving direction for daily concerns and the unique assignment he created you to complete. This may not be an audible expression, but as you read Scripture or receive personal spiritual advice,
your inner spirit will become aware of the presence of God, enabling
you to discern the path the Holy Spirit is leading you to take.

It is essential that we spend time with God outside corporate worship
at church. Quiet time with God should be a daily occurrence, but so
often this is not the case. After all the rituals, socializing at church, and
doing business in the marketplace, what happens when you are alone at
home? Are you communicating with God? Are you making time for
private spiritual development? God created you for fellowship with
himself; when you actively seek his presence, he will guide and enable
you to synchronize your life physically, emotionally, and spiritually.

Pausing amid the chaos of life can help you grow spiritually and dramatically change the course of your life. When you pause long enough, you can align with God's leading and be even further enlightened and awakened regarding God's plans, purposes, and kingdom assignments for your life. Your assignments may include family, occupation, and ministry on different levels. God knows and has your blueprint; he wants to reveal it to you as you press pause with him.

Regardless of your present relationship with God, you can intensify your Christian walk by pausing on purpose and implementing quiet time. This will renew your faith, build hope, help you find peace, and position you to receive favor from God and man to live as a champion every day. The influence of your covenant relationship with God can be demonstrated on earth, affecting your life and the lives of others as you develop a habit of daily personal quiet time.

SPIRITUAL HOMEOSTASIS

The increased amount of stress Americans are under is contributing to a variety of health problems, but few know how to get a real handle on their out-of-control lives. As a longtime medical professional, I've observed that people are out of control because they are burned out and cannot stay ahead of the game. They are constantly pushing and struggling because they think they are in control of the results of their lives, believing that "If I don't do it, I know it won't be done."

We have committed our limited time to church, work, community, family, and professional activities, attempting to meet multiple deadlines and various obligations. By doing so, we risk our well-being, and so many of us are experiencing the dangerous symptoms of burnout in our emotions and relationships. This high-speed lifestyle also depletes the capacity of our spiritual relationship with God and compromises our daily activities, decision-making insight, and creativity.

There was a season when I was juggling caring for my family, working grueling shifts as a physician's assistant, participating in various community activities, writing, and speaking—all during a two-year journey of surgery and chemotherapy after being diagnosed with breast cancer—where God taught me to stop, think, and breathe. When I didn't, I experienced personal "power outages," leading to a nearly complete shutdown on multiple levels. This diagnosis of "hurry syndrome" fragmented my life even more, as I subconsciously ignored signals to pause and redirect my time.

Pausing allows us to realign our internal priorities and make choices that agree with God's purpose for our lives, including wise use of our time and schedules. It rids us of unhealthy striving to be and do everything society suggests as a path to purpose and worldly success. We have free will to determine and act on the need to slow down and hear the voice of God. This leads us to greater enjoyment of life's blessings, abundance even amid troubles, and success with far less stress. It is up to us. God is loving and understands our human behavior; thus, he is long-suffering and waiting patiently until we are ready to come and sit in his presence to learn from him.

Applying the right tools to maintain spiritual balance is crucial to our well-being. They assist in developing healthy moral consciousness, decision-making, godly living, and success in the marketplace. Understanding this empowers us to lead a life of harmony and balance with God and man. In my experience as a healthcare practitioner and professor, I know all too well that maintaining homeostasis is vital to natural health and life. In the spiritual realm, God, in his infinite wisdom, has provided mechanisms to correct imbalances regarding our spiritual homeostasis.

Why is this important? If the body does not recognize a change in normal regulation of its functions, sickness and even death can ensue. Likewise, when our spirit is not in harmony with God's Holy Spirit, there are signals in place to aid in discernment of the consequences of our choices and behaviors. At that point, we can willfully continue in our own strength or adjust and align with God's direction.

MECHANISMS FOR PHYSICAL AND
SPIRITUAL HOMEOSTASIS

Let's examine some basic concepts associated with natural, human body homeostasis and convert their usage into the context of spiritual homeostasis.

Negative feedback to restore homeostasis. Negative feedback is a mechanism that identifies an undesired change and corrects it with counteractions. This opposite action is accomplished by the control center messaging a hormone or organ to reduce the agent's effects of imbalance. This occurs through a signal that slows and stops the unwanted change and restores equilibrium.

Biological example of negative feedback. In the case of diabetes, when blood glucose (sugar) increases above normal, the control center sends a message to the pancreas to release insulin to lower blood glucose, returning it to normal (equilibrium) levels. If the pancreas is malfunctioning, the body will require insulin to be injected to restore blood glucose equilibrium.

Spiritual example of negative feedback. After days, months, or years of little time with God, our spirit becomes nearly empty of the presence of God. Jesus intercedes with the Father for us, and if we respond to the call of correction and draw near, he will draw near to us to correct unwanted behavior. The opposite actions of prayer, reading, and journaling counteract the disconnection with God. Then spiritual fatigue is removed, and the freshness of joy strengthens us to move forward.

Positive feedback to restore homeostasis. This mechanism recognizes an increase in a substance, and a signal is sent to the control center that validates an abnormality. A message is sent out to correct the abnormal imbalance, increasing a substance (for example a hormone) until the abnormal imbalance slows and stops, returning the body's function to equilibrium.

Biological example of positive feedback. When a woman is pregnant, initiation of labor is triggered by the hormone oxytocin, which is released and increases, sending a message to start uterine contractions.

The hormone continues to increase, as does pain and the opening of the cervix, until the baby is delivered, and under normal conditions the body's equilibrium of hormones is restored. In the case of induced labor, the woman is given increased amounts of a synthetic version of oxytocin, known as Pitocin, to stimulate uterine contraction until delivery of the baby.

Spiritual example of positive feedback. The more time away from private worship, the less guilty we may feel. It's as if we no longer depend on God and instead accomplish goals and dreams without God. We become emotionally fatigued, with signs of irritability and less patience. Have you ever felt like that? But the more we pause in prayer, the more we gain self-control to find time with God and correct our spiritual homeostasis. Discipline for spiritual development can seem hard when changing a habit; in the beginning, regular prayer, reading, and journaling can be hard work when we have been out of control with no time for God.

The concept of spiritual homeostasis is a state of being that navigates us into the path of righteous living, God-consciousness, and maturity, with a sense of positive well-being. In many cases, spiritual homeostasis acts like the leveler that helps us to align our will to the purpose of God. Think about how many times you have looked at a picture unevenly tilted on the wall and stopped to straighten it so that it was balanced. As Christians, there are times when we are misaligned with the ways of God and need an adjustment: The same annoying feeling of displeasure with a crooked wall hanging is prompted in our spirit—but how often do we stop to adjust our lives to the ways and plans of God? Anytime we detour from the path of righteousness, we know it, and we have a choice to follow the redirection of the Holy Spirit. We must listen to what the Holy Spirit is saying to us.

Friends, when we make room for sacred reading, conversation with Father God, and reflective listening, we become in sync with the will of God. Obedience, trust, and walking in faith become easier the more we are in the private chambers of worship. Take a break here and revisit the mechanisms God has in place to maintain spiritual homeostasis, to avoid derailment or misalignment with his will for your life. An imbalance of spiritual homeostasis discloses how messy or unbalanced one's life is . . . just like a tilted picture on the wall. Which example of spiritual homeostasis would be beneficial for you now? Why?

CULTIVATE OUR SPIRITS

Moving beyond misalignment—that state of being twisted, unbalanced, or fragmented that women often overcorrect to stabilize themselves—we can cultivate our spirits in a slow, steady pace. This positively impacts our confidence and emotional fatigue, allowing us to show up in a more excellent way at home, in church, or in the marketplace. In this book we cannot teach a full lesson about the Proverbs 31 woman, but we can highlight how her life exhorts women today to seek God first. He wants women who will give him their all, not the cold leftovers of fatigue, irritability, doubt, or fear.

Discerning the difference between positive and negative feedback can take time and effort. God loves us and wants to spend time with us to teach us the way of holiness and to help us understand and differentiate his ways from the ways of the world. With his help, we can travel the narrow road, which ultimately leads to heaven, instead of the wide road of sin and disobedience, which results in hell and eternal separation from God.

For example, at one point I was discipling a young woman new to Christianity. She honestly loved her new relationship with God and was maturing spiritually. One day, she shared that she could not understand why she felt uncomfortable and that something was wrong when she went home, now that she had accepted Jesus into her life. When I gently asked, she told me she lived with her boyfriend and their children, and she admitted she didn't know what fornication was.

We spent time talking about the definition of fornication. She determined on her own that the Holy Spirit was teaching her that it was not appropriate to have a sexual relationship or live together in the same house as unmarried individuals. This is an example of the Holy Spirit's positive feedback resetting the standard of consciousness and realigning conduct for righteous obedience. After praying for several days, she asked the young man to move out of the home because of her new decision to be a Christian. And he did so without any argument or altercation. He admitted recognizing a change in her life but did not know what to do. After several months, he returned and asked her to marry him, and they became husband and wife. God is faithful to reward obedience.

If she had continued living with the young man while remaining unmarried, it would have been a self-reinforcing choice supporting negative feedback outcomes. The reaction of continuing to move toward the opposite set standard would have unfavorably exacerbated her condition of discomfort. But instead she embraced time in the presence of God daily—reading, praying, and listening reflectively— which triggered conviction in her heart. In addition, having a compassionate listener to trust is another way she was learning how to hear and understand the voice of God in discipleship.

What is the Holy Spirit nudging you to change for improved spiritual health? God is speaking . . . will you choose to obey? Press pause and listen to the voice of God in the pages of the Bible, in sermons, in a song of praise and worship, in the "still, small voice" of your heart, or in discipleship relationships with other believers. God uses multiple approaches to give you his love and blessings for an abundant life on earth and eternal joy with him in heaven.

Spiritual homeostasis is maintained or can be reset in the peaceful quiescence of pause—time with God to gain his perspective on what is most essential. Pressing pause is anticultural in that it creates a distance from other worldviews and social trends that use various media in attempts to be the dominant voice influencing humanity. Can you hear God calling? "Come away, my beloved" is the Holy Spirit's invitation to pause from the world's nonstop activity as frequently as possible (Song of Songs 8:14).

There is an answer to our ever-increasing busyness and it's as old as creation. If you feel like your life is getting out of control, if it seems obligations dictate every minute of your day, or if you lack the focus you need to reflect and let God reset the priorities for your day in quiet times, then you need to press the button and pause on purpose. I like to use the acronym POP to remind myself to pause on purpose, an action step that prevents and resolves internal stressful upheavals, poor decisions, and external explosive behaviors. If you begin your day in the quiet presence of God while reading or meditating, you will be better able to store the Word of God in your heart and mind and retrieve it when needed. This will grant you peace and confidence to meet the situations and challenges experienced throughout the day.

PAUSE ON PURPOSE 2

WAITING TO EXHALE

David was greatly distressed because the men were talking of stoning him; each one was bitter in spirit because of his sons and daughters. But David found strength in the LORD his God. – 1 SAMUEL 30:6

Responsibilities at home, work, and community can bring great joy when tasks are completed and everyone you serve is happy. But when crises and challenges affect different areas of our lives in what feels like a domino effect, we can become nearly consumed with despair. While working as unto the Lord in a competitive environment, I was often challenged to retaliate in my strength. I had to press in and practice what I had been teaching—to stop, think, and breathe instead of holding toxicity inside. I had to stop and release it to God in times of quiet prayer and listen for instructions throughout the day. Walking around the building on breaks and reflecting on the truth of what God said about the situations encouraged me.

In a moment of loss of capital and family, David's life was threatened. He needed direction to recover the people's trust and all that his enemies took away. Surrounded by masses of grieving people, David encouraged himself in God. He had a relationship with God because he paused and began to worship and praise him, regaining strength as he called for the ephod. In this space, he sought the will of God and strategies to recover from the setback.

During his time with the Father, David inquired about the next steps. God directed him to move forward in battle. Throughout the journey, we see David maintained an awareness of God's leading. He obtained clarity to discern the physical needs of his two hundred men left behind. He acquired favor with a servant of the enemy who led them to the Amalekites' camp. David's battle plan was successful, recovering all that was lost. He did not let his win create insensitivity to the two hundred men who did not go to battle, but he was compassionate, sharing the spoils with them. Indeed, we can have favor with God and man.

Even in the middle of working in toxicity, God will provide a fresh wind if we breathe in the pureness of the Holy Spirit. How long can we absorb carbon dioxide (CO_2) in our bodies before requiring fresh oxygen (O_2)? God's design of homeostasis for respiration is to exhale toxic stress and inhale renewed peace in his presence.

Reflection: Breathing comes naturally, without our awareness, but as soon as we hold our breath too long, the stress in the body forces us to pause and exhale. What do you need to release?

Prayer: God, throughout this day, help me be aware that you are present, and I don't have to wait until I am overwhelmed, frustrated, or in doubt to call on you. I can pause anytime with you, exhaling every concern and resting in knowing. Amen.

3

STOP. BREATHE. THINK.

I remember the days of old; I meditate on all Your doings;
I ponder the work of Your hands. I spread forth my hands to You;
my soul thirsts after You like a thirsty land [for water].
Selah [pause, and calmly think about that]!

PSALM 143:5-6 AMPC

SITTING AT A TRAFFIC LIGHT, I glanced at what I call my mobile desk: the passenger seat of my car. I noticed my planner and realized I had rushed out of the house to begin my day without first communing with my Father God. I had checked my social media, started the crock pot, exercised, drank twenty ounces of water, dressed, grabbed a change of clothes for an evening event, and was out the door. As I went on my way, I kept thinking I had forgotten something important but could not grasp it. I went down my lists, both written and in my memory, and it became apparent that I had checked off quiet time with God but had not actually spent proper time with him. After this nudge from deep within, I pulled my car over and looked in my lavender journal, only to discover I had not written any "love notes to my Daddy" for the day. It was then I recognized the missing piece.

I immediately parked my car in the lot of a local grocery store and stopped to pray and reflect on Matthew 6:33, "But seek first his kingdom and his righteousness, and all these things will be given to you as well." This passage served as a spiritual signal to remind me to slow down to prevent further abnormal behavior that left unchecked would adversely affect my relationship with the Lord. I could have chosen to disregard this notification; however, when I realized what was missing in my morning, I had two options: (1) pause with God now, or (2) decide to catch up with him later on and possibly forget again. After parking lot time with God, I was energized and spiritually prepared for the day.

Many Christians have allowed the demands of their busy schedules to diminish the quality and quantity of the time they devote to God. They attempt to beat the clock as they meet the demands of work, ministry, and family—as moments with God fall to the wayside. Others do make time for personal time in prayer, Bible reading, and reflection, but it is done in such a legalistic fashion that it becomes drudgery. The result for both groups is that they fail to develop a naturally authentic approach to prayer. A heart for a relationship with our Creator, the source of all we are and all we can accomplish, seeks to encounter the Spirit of God. A fruitful life as a Christian requires time management with God in mind, blocking time in one's schedule to meet in his presence. Periods of quiet are intentional acts of surrender to God. It is not an action out of duty or forced routine. The act of surrender of time positions the bowing of one's heart to engage—the God of the universe, the source of all life and provision.

Beginning our day with quiet time keeps us on the path to our life goals and divine purpose. Pausing on purpose prevents us from being driven by social trends and instead being led by the Holy Spirit to pursue the will of God for our life. The concept of "seeking God first" has been lost amid the rat race of achievement. The idea that we must accomplish our goals by any means necessary is a famous mantra—yes, even to the point of damaging our health and relationships with family, friends, and God. During my unexpected pit stop that day, I remembered what the Bible says in Proverbs 3:6—that if we acknowledge God in all our ways, he will direct our path. Are you willing to follow the leader who knows our future?

In this verse, we find insight into why we must press pause to spend time with God. Moments of spiritual intimacy lead to an increasing consciousness regarding his presence; we obtain direction for making everyday decisions, and it prompts us to live balanced lives. Our lives depend on these moments to stop, think, and breathe—to rest and reset the spirit, mind, and body. We know that physiologically, when we stop breathing, we die. But equally important, when we deprive ourselves of spiritual nutrients, we become disconnected and can yield to temptation easier. Maintaining a healthy and godly lifestyle results from getting to know the character of God. Suppose we ignore the internal spiritual homeostatic sensor alert too many times: in that case, our spiritual health will decline, ending in spiritual disconnection due to lack of private and public time with God ... requiring relational resuscitation.

My prayer is that you will become more attentive to your relationship with God within a busy world of activities. It is my hope that you will become deliberate about managing your time, including spiritual meals. Begin setting aside short intervals for prayer and reading, so that you don't neglect what appears to be invisible—God our source and the giver of all when we learn to seek him.

WHAT EXACTLY IS QUIET TIME?

Quiet time is a personal form of worship. It is a time of prayer, thanksgiving, praise, Bible reading, and meditation. It is also an opportunity to connect with God each day to learn what to to expect from your covenant and to be able to trust him. Pausing in quiet time is a special time of personal fellowship—a space for private spiritual growth. Quiet time is where one goes to learn the character of God, strengthen one's faith, and trust in the Word.

The term *quiet time* is often described in these ways:

- spending time alone with God with no distractions
- talking with God
- reading the Bible and praying
- being in the presence of God
- meditating on God's Word
- morning meditations and devotions
- sabbath moments
- devotional and journal time

Although these are all good descriptions, a fruitful quiet time, simply put, consists of communing (connecting) with God. The acts of prayer, worship, and praise are pathways that bridge you over to him in the spirit. These encounters of private fellowship are building blocks of spiritual maturity. When your spirit, mind, and body embrace God's presence, there is two-way communication experienced between you and the Father.

Receiving direction for our lives is one of the benefits of quiet time, but the real purpose is to maintain a healthy relationship. In other words, fellowship is a form of communication that protects our covenant connection with the Father. Genesis 1:26-27 gives us insight into why fellowship with him is so important to God. In that passage, God makes a profound statement:

> Then God said, "Let us make mankind in our image, in our likeness, so that they may rule over the fish in the sea and the birds in the sky, over the livestock and all the wild animals, and over all the creatures that move along the ground." So God created mankind in his own image, in the image of God he created them; male and female he created them.

God made all creatures of the earth, according to their kind, for the purpose of relationships. In his perfect design, he created man and woman in his image and likeness for perfect fellowship with him (and each other). Teaching the significance of fellowship and the progression of how to touch the heart of God is dear to me. The key is the willingness to practice time management. Lock in dedicated time with him so that you are not rushing because you are double-booked. Undivided intimacy builds a trusted relationship and spiritual growth. In stillness—the fellowship of pause—we learn how to acquire and effectively use our God-given birthrights as Christians for our families, ministries, and in the marketplace.

The fact that God desires our fellowship is perhaps one of the most unique concepts conveyed through the Scriptures. It is almost incomprehensible to think that God gets great pleasure in relationship and fellowship with us mere humans. A close relationship with the Lord results from quality time together.

KEEP QUIET TIME REGULAR, NOT RIGID

Allocating time with God does not mean you must set strict "God time" and meet him at the same time, same length of time, and in the same place each day. Although the same time and place are good, we live in a time of history that doesn't always accommodate those guidelines. That thinking is more about religious legalism than pursuing a personal relationship. I find it easier to start my quiet time early in the morning with a designated time and prepared space, but just as there are times when I can spend nearly all day in a place of worship, spending less than an hour or ten minutes can be equally effective. It is a matter of the heart. When possible I recommend that this focused time occur before you start your day. It sets the stage for better productivity.

My brief pit stop pause in the grocery store parking lot was refreshing, and I gained clarity for my day, just as if I were home in my prepared space for quiet time. That experience taught me how easily Christians can ritualize when and where they connect with God. Does God want time with us? Yes. But not to pray empty prayers or write in our journals to mark off the time as yet another completed task. God loves us and wants us to walk with him in this life as we fulfill his designs and purposes in this world; he does not want to be called on and used only in an emergency when we feel our natural abilities and intellect are ineffective.

An example of God demonstrating his desire for a relationship with humanity is in Genesis 3:8: "[Adam and Eve] heard the sound of the LORD God as he was walking in the garden in the cool of the day, and they hid from the LORD God among the trees of the garden." Before their disobedience and fall, Adam and Eve met regularly with God at appointed times. But there is more we can take away from this narrative of Adam and Eve. Considering they were in a relationship with God because of their fellowship in the Garden of Eden, think about why they hid from God rather than continuing their regular visit when they heard him walking. It is evident that Adam and Eve knew they had done something wrong, since they knew their actions would make God unhappy with them.

Even under grace, many of us allow our shortcomings and over-whelming schedules to keep us from building and maintaining a quality personal relationship with the God of our lives, just as Adam and Eve did. He is the One who knows the best schedule for us and has the perfect creative strategies and plans for us to accomplish our dreams and goals. Yet all too often, we do not plan adequate time in his presence as a daily routine to build a relationship with the God of mercy and love. When we press the pause button and "facetime" with God, we will learn to know God as Father and who we are as his children.

God meets us where we are whenever we reach out to him. A relationship with God is based on a personal acceptance of Christ as Savior. The gift of salvation is available for all who accept him, and it comes with the responsibility to nurture the relationship if we want to know God fully. Seeking God the Father in our quiet time—whenever and wherever that is—strengthens us for life's journey. As the Bible says in 1 Chronicles 16:11 (HCSB), "Search for the LORD and for His strength; seek His face always."

On the other hand, how many of us have a testimony like Adam and Eve, when we are in error and don't want to be in God's presence, even when that is what we need the most? We may sense God's presence amid all we do but shrug him off and say, "I will fill in time with the Lord tonight before bed or tomorrow morning when I am more focused." Instead, we fall asleep exhausted and oversleep the next day. Yet God still desires intimacy with us. How awesome it is to read in Genesis 3:9 that God was still in pursuit of Adam despite his sin: "The LORD God called to [Adam], 'Where are you?'" Do you hear God calling you? He misses time with you.

Consider this anonymous statement: "I am convinced that God does not wish us to neglect rightful work to pray. But it is equally certain that we might work better and do more work if we gave less time to work and more to prayer."[1] Many spend years striving to reach personal and professional goals but do not prioritize time to abide in God's presence. We should always find space and time for God. In the words of Jesus, "Few things are needed—or indeed only one. Mary has chosen what is better, and it will not be taken away from her" (Luke 10:42). We must do as Mary did and spend time at the feet of Jesus.

"Stop, Breathe, and Think" (SBT) is a phrase that assists individuals and groups to take a few minutes of their day to find peace of mind and a bit of calm in their frantic schedules. It gives power to check in determining the self-location of their actions, thoughts, and feelings. SBT is a type of alarm that signals and guides the practice of mindful exercises, such as deep breathing and reflection. While the SBT concept is popular among New Age practitioners,[2] it points to a truth that can be found in Scripture. Mindfulness is not a new practice. Christians were instructed to always be mindful of God's Word, as we are encouraged to delight in the law and meditate on it day and night (Psalm 1:2). The psalmist later proclaims his commitment to meditate and consider the ways of God (Psalm 119:15). Surely, you cannot be in full motion when you honor those commitments.

The Bible shows us that the Father doesn't expect us to do anything he would not do for humanity. In 1 Chronicles 16:15, the Bible teaches us he is *mindful*: "He remembers his covenant forever, the promise he made, for a thousand generations." Those who keep their eyes on the Lord will be blessed in due season (Psalm 145:15-16).

You can practice pressing pause and commit 1 Chronicles 16:15 to your heart, mind, and soul, knowing full well God will keep his promise. Give yourself a gift by including slow, deep breaths as you read and pray, to take full advantage of being present in any press pause moment.

QUIET RESOLVES ISSUES OF THE SOUL

As a recovered performance-driven individual, who loved servanthood to the point of not realizing an addiction to people pleasing, I wanted to make everyone happy. It was through learning to press pause in quiet time, journaling my emotions, and praying that I discovered the source of my hurry. It was in quiet that I was free, that although my work was good work, God wanted me to care for myself. During one of my silent retreats, the Scripture "Everything should be done in a fitting and orderly way"(1 Corinthians 14:40) spoke loudly to me. Let's unpack that: God knows the plan for our lives, and if he knows when, what, and where we should do a thing, then it is easier to seek the Master Planner for instructions first in prayer. The best way to obtain direction is to seek him to know when to do all things in decency and order so that we can avoid heartache, anxiety, depression, and health conditions.

Through learning to examine my emotions, I began to immediately identify women who are suffering with anxiety, depression, and other health conditions, in many cases secondary to succumbing to the effect of allostatic load, reaching a point of fatigue, and some reaching breakdown. In this state, you begin to believe every lie the devil whispers: You are a failure, unloved, being used, and a waste of time. Friends, pause is the cure to striving and being performance-driven as a people pleaser. Sure, you are talented, have many skills, and enjoy what you are doing at work, church, home, and community, but remember in all you do, ask the Father, "Is it your will to say yes now?" Trust me, he will answer. This is why implementing a pause to regularly stop, think, and breathe is empowering to every decision you make . . . even if it is in the local grocery store parking lot.

Lord, I thank you for the power to transcend these pages and touch my sisters deep in their souls, in the core of every hurt, disappointment; feelings of defeat, comparison, anxiousness; and belief in the lies of Satan. Father, thank you for your touch of love and healing of their every concern, as hope is renewed and vision for purpose clarified. Let them know it is not over; this is the beginning of a new season.

PAUSE ON PURPOSE 3

TENDING YOUR SOUL

But Daniel resolved not to defile himself with the royal food and wine, and he asked the chief official for permission not to defile himself this way. – DANIEL 1:8

Pursuing the American dream held me captive until my late 40s. I was a hostage to hurry and driven by an unseen force that compelled me to meet the demands of career, church, and community service with a family. It was eye-opening to learn I was distracted from what I preached and taught—quiet time for my soul. I recognized that I was choosing to spend less time in God's presence. It was as if I convinced myself that everything I did substituted for time with God. Sure, I was reading my Bible, praying, and serving humankind. Still, the true essence of my relationship with God was fractured, and I felt distant from him. The void began to impact all areas of my life.

Competitive societal trends, expectations, and the pursuit of the best through our skills, gifts, and creativity continue to be the world's driving force. Women of influence can be found in the home and marketplace, giving and filling tall orders from morning to evening. The internal whistle to pause goes unheard during the rush of the day. It becomes so easy to lose our God-given identity to perform for the prizes and appreciation of the world, pursuing what humankind thinks will bring happiness and fulfillment.

Let's take a moment and look at Daniel. Although a teenager when taken into captivity by the Babylonians, he remembered the importance of time with God in prayer. He chose to honor God by not defiling his body, which preserved his identity in a foreign land. Daniel had many tasks and responsibilities like others in captivity, but Daniel continued to pause three times daily to pray as he was taught. Oppositions came to his schedule, yet he decided to continue tending to his soul, and God blessed his obedience.

Daniel did not perceive relationship maintenance as a rule of drudgery, punishment, or control. Pausing for time with God is a solution to the complications of "hurry syndrome." In other words, a pause is an exit from the fast pace to reset. Why reset? To effectively respond, react, and make quality judgments that please God, even if not always pleasing others. Pausing honors God's direction from the Word and helps us make wise decisions that gain favor with God. Daniel's life teaches us that relationship building with God is sacrificial.

We are here not only to transform the world but also to be transformed.[3] —Parker J. Palmer

Reflection: Where in your day can you pause and nurture your soul?

Prayer: Lord, grant me insight into your purposes and plan for my life today as I obey and honor you.

4

BELOVED, COME AWAY

So there is a special rest still waiting for the people of God.

HEBREWS 4:9 NLT

GOD ESTABLISHED THE MODEL for balanced living in spirit, mind, and body. He knew the children of Israel would not know how to rest after their four hundred years of labor as enslaved people, so he established the Sabbath as a day of remembrance and rest, just as he took a day of rest from his labors of creation in Genesis 2:2-3. Although practiced differently by Jews and Christians, the Sabbath rest that God set in place is still meaningful today. Godly living and abundant life coincide with intentional efforts to schedule time in our day or devote an entire day to reflection on God's goodness. Prayer, meditation, and Scripture reading can clear our minds spiritually and keep us aware of the necessity to care for ourselves mentally and physically—as our bodies are the temple of the Holy Spirit.

All too often we associate Christianity and church membership with servanthood, event participation, and other religious activities and use them as a substitute for spending direct time with God, thus forgetting our intimacy with God and self-care. The institution of rest on our personal sabbath establishes boundaries to prevent burnout, enables us to maintain an individual and corporate relationship with

God, and helps us learn to seek and trust God for wisdom and guidance personally. *Sabbath rest* is another interchangeable name for *press pause*, and it creates a quiet mind to refuel our spirit in the presence of God.

As the Israelites obeyed God in observance of the Sabbath, they learned to trust him as Jehovah Jireh, the One who would provide for their needs, even on the days they did not work. They took time with family, teaching their children about Yahweh as they reflected on his goodness to their people throughout the generations. Even in our modern era, spending time with God is vital for our effectiveness in fulfilling his commission while living day to day in a world of demands. Implementing moments of pause in sabbath rest draws us nearer to God and prevents life's hindrances from pushing us away from our Father. The closer we become to God, the more we will recognize the presence of the Holy Spirit. Today, pause in any form of sabbath rest that brings us in remembrance of the goodness of God.[1]

The Hebrew word for breath, *ruakh*, is also defined as "wind" or "spirit," but in a religious context, it refers to the divine inspiration or divine voice of God as the Holy Spirit. The Greek word for spirit (*pneuma*) has similar meanings.[2] In those moments, we pause to stop, breathe, and think so we will experience God's guidance and divine inspiration for work, rest, reflection, and recreational components of our journey in life. Pressing pause in daily activity allows us to sense the sacred download of God's Spirit as we discern the direction for our life, as well as how to model the character of God. It is the will of God that we live a life of wholeness—nothing missing or broken.

As a medical practitioner, I want people to realize how important it is to be spiritually, emotionally, and physically healthy to fulfill their purpose. To begin balanced living, we can pause to renew our spirit in God's presence. Let me challenge you to practice James 4:8, which tells us, "Come near to God, and he will come near to you." This can be done by committing to stop every day at some point to pray, read, reflect, and journal about your time with the Lord. The length of time that you spend with God is not as important as simply choosing to press pause. Your time with God will grow as you begin to experience the benefits of knowing him more intimately.

HIS YOKE IS EASY

Speaking at a retreat one summer, I was talking about how intimacy with God was like being "yoked" with God. Nervousness got the best of me, and I mistakenly began to relate egg yolks to sharing our burden with Jesus. Yes, I even described how the egg spreads to make contact with the frying pan, similarly to the Spirit embracing and binding with us when we pause. Then I asked the women to imagine being "yoked" with Jesus as they experience confidence and assurance knowing we are "yoked" with the great I Am. I asked them to see themselves achieving goals and dreams while intermingling with God's Son. What a mess they probably envisioned! The attendees praised God during the presentation—that was love in action. Afterward, a kind sister came and informed me that I had used the wrong word; it should have been *yoke*. I told her that the Spirit helped them get the point, even though I found the *yolk* example funny when I thought about it later. Our being yoked with God is ever more powerful.

Answering the call to fellowship with God should not become a burden that wears us out as if we were wearing a heavy *yoke*—a device used to carry a heavy load. Matthew 11:28-30 tells us that when we respond to Jesus' call to come to him, he will give us rest: "Come to me, all you who are weary and burdened, and I will give you rest. Take my yoke upon you and learn from me, for I am gentle and humble in heart, and you will find rest for your souls. For my yoke is easy and my burden is light."

The yoke Jesus spoke of was not the tradition and ordinances the Pharisees and Sadducees used like a rod to force acceptable behavior. Today's version of this yoke may include overcommitting ourselves, functioning in God's permissive (instead of his perfect) will, or being totally out of God's will. Yoked animals were joined as such to increase strength to get a job done. Imagine being so connected to God and allowing him to support, guide, and strengthen you as both of you complete a task together. Jesus is offering companionship through intimacy to lessen the load of the burdens of life.

Many of the yokes we bear are self-inflicted, the result of saying yes too often and no not often enough, making compromises with our time, and creating walls of religious routines that block our ability to receive what God wants to do in our hearts and lives. Sometimes, responding to the call to rest requires us to stop one or more activities to develop discipline, rest, and faithfulness in communion with him instead of only seeking God in need. The journey becomes easy and restful in the presence of God, a place where we can discern the path we are to take each day.

The yoke on a pair of oxen serves as a connector to aid in guidance and lessen the burden of their weight. Similarly, we become paired with the Holy Spirit as we let him support and direct us, reducing the load on our journey.

Press pause in God's presence and let him lift your burdens. The more time we spend with God, the more we reflect his image on the earth and acquire clarity of direction. People will see him in our lives. Think about your coworkers, friends, family, and neighbors. Do they see you as an example of Christ?

LEARNING TO PAUSE FROM JESUS

There is no doubt that the Son of God in human form became physically tired as he traveled throughout Galilee, healing the sick, liberating the demon-possessed, and ministering to the needs of multitudes as his works became more widely known. His pattern was to rise early in the morning to pray and commune with his Father in a solitary place, even when he was likely mentally, spiritually, and physically drained from ministering. We see this in Mark 1:35, which says, "Very early in the morning, while it was still dark, Jesus got up, left the house and went off to a solitary place, where he prayed." Read that passage again, and note the three things the Son of God did on purpose. It is clear that he (1) woke up very early in the morning, (2) went to a solitary place, and (3) prayed. He did all this before taking on other tasks or activities that day.

The purpose of Bible reading and prayer is to enhance the mental capacity to focus on God, to see through fresh eyes for positive aspects of life and build character. You might be in a hostile work environment, required to make life-and-death decisions, managing the finances of a large corporation, having domestic concerns, or even starting your own small business or ministry. Each of these scenarios and an infinite number of other situations require steadiness of thought and emotions. Taking the time to pause on purpose affords you breathing room to re-center your focus on God for guidance. Most notably, Bible reading enhances our understanding of living as children of God.

It is a privilege to draw near to God as he draws close to you. Whatever you call your time with God, you must pause on purpose; it cannot be accomplished in motion. It is crucial to recognize that spending time with God is essential for our daily living and to the success of our work for God's kingdom.

THE GAP OF SPIRITUAL ADULTERY AND IDOLATRY

When we neglect building our relationship with God, we begin to form and prioritize relationships with false idols such as our businesses, ministries, careers, fitness, other people, and material things. When our time excludes God, we commit spiritual adultery. We confess we are Christians, covenant partners, followers of Christ, or born again—all of which indicate a commitment; however, the personal relationship with God is neglected. Idolatry is committed when the living and true God is replaced by any other noun—person, place, or thing—as our highest priority. Both spiritual adultery and idolatry can form a gap so vast that the distance between us and our Father God eventually leads to spiritual death. The evidence of death is visible in many ways: loss of appetite for spiritual activities, limited vision and creativity, isolation, a sense of void, and decreased productivity.

I have friends who are successful but do not acknowledge or even believe in God. Thus, one might argue that worldly success is not based on God. However, these individuals are constantly driven yet often feel a sense of emptiness. Not long ago, one of them admitted that they had everything they wanted, yet they still felt something was missing. As Christians, we are instructed to seek God first. How does seeking God first connect with a better quality of life? God foresaw that we would live in a world filled with many so-called pharaohs, which can be anything that drives us beyond reason, such as stressful work with intense demands. Therefore, he instituted the Sabbath to remind and encourage us to rest. Even with all of the advances of technology in work-related tasks, much of humanity still neglects their relationship with God, instead choosing to work longer and harder. The availability of technology does not always lighten the workload nor loosen the hands of some taskmasters. Far too often the system pushes us harder to exceed previous levels of productivity and success, creating further spiritual absenteeism from the One who is our Covenant Partner—God alone.

Spiritual absenteeism affects our destiny. It may not appear this way initially, but it becomes evident over time in our personal lives and work. If we honestly look at our local communities and the world at large as documented through the lens of the media, we see an increasing disconnect from God. Even among professing Christians, we can see the results of neglecting time with God and giving other things more of our attention. This lack of singleness of heart for one's relationship with God contributes to a sense of unfulfillment amid success; there is also much less tolerance and compassion for other human lives. The increased inequalities seen across the social injustices in our world can be attributed to being self-centered while spending minimal (if any) time cultivating a relationship in the presence of God. As we learn the character of God, we begin to demonstrate his will on the earth, modeling compassion, kindness, joy, and a giving heart, changing the world one person at a time.

A passage in the book of Psalms speaks to our end when we disconnect from the Lord. Take a moment to read Psalm 73:22-28 as it is translated in the Christian Standard Bible:

I was stupid and didn't understand; I was an unthinking animal toward you. Yet I am always with you; you hold my right hand. You guide me with your counsel, and afterward you will take me up in glory. Who do I have in heaven but you? And I desire nothing on earth but you. My flesh and my heart may fail, but God is the strength of my heart, my portion forever. Those far from you will certainly perish; you destroy all who are unfaithful to you. But as for me, God's presence is my good. I have made the Lord GOD my refuge, so I can tell about all you do.

Pausing long enough to stop, breathe, and think is a way of preserving the presence of God in our lives, positively impacting our world as we honor our relationship with the Lord. Learning to press the pause button takes intentional effort. Relationship building with God enhances *our* character if we embrace *his* character to help us model the kingdom and truly live successful lives on earth.

Three familiar Scripture passages can help to achieve mental clarity for success in a godly manner. Grab a Bible, take a deep breath, and read the following passages slowly. God wants all of you: Joshua 1:8; Romans 12:1-5; and James 4:7-8.

We grow in wisdom as Jesus did when we press pause throughout the day to fellowship with our Father. Spending consistent time in God's presence on purpose is a front line of defense for Christians. First Peter 5:8 reminds us, "Be alert and of sober mind. Your enemy the devil prowls around like a roaring lion looking for someone to devour." To be vigilant is to be alert, and to have a sober mind speaks to being on guard and protective of our relationship with God, our place of righteousness in Christ, and the benefits of being his joint heirs. In return, he protects our destiny, calms our anxiety, and fulfills our purpose on earth. All of this begins in our quiet time with God.

In the heat of your day, pause long enough to read, pray, think, and listen for the leading of the Holy Spirit. Charles Swindoll said, "Make a plan now to keep a daily appointment with God. The enemy will tell you to set it aside, but you must carve out the time. If you are too busy to meet with the Lord, friend, then you are simply too busy."[3]

PAUSE ON PURPOSE 4

WHO'S CALLING?

Then Peter called to him, "Lord, if it's really you,
tell me to come to you, walking on the water." — MATTHEW 14:28 (NLT)

On a Sunday morning, speaking at a women's prison, the title of my message was "Who's Calling?" One of my colaborers in Christ, Sonya Bryant, kept reminding me of that theme as I continued to bloom in ministry. She's since gone home to be with the Lord, but I can still see her in my mind and remember that every time she saw me, she would whisper with a smile, "Who's calling?"

The desire to say yes to all the voices, requests, opportunities, and offers in response to so many needs can result in confusion and weariness, diverting you from God's specific purpose for your life. I know I have been there. While doing life, I was blindsided by a crisis of faith that stormed around me like a category-four tornado. I had answered God's call when he said to come, but I rushed ahead too fast, relying on my limited vision instead of looking and moving through the lens of God's plans.

In Matthew 14, after Jesus fed the hungry in the middle of a crisis and heard about his cousin John the Baptist's death, Jesus asked the disciples to cross over to the other side of the lake. Jesus paused on the mountainside to rest and commune with his Father. Later, Jesus walked on water to join the disciples. While the disciples had seen many miracles, they were afraid when they saw an image walking on water at night.

Once they realized it was Jesus, Peter asked to come out on the water with him. How often have you seen the Lord's hand move in your life through healing, at work, or in your family? Then seeing his power, you ask God to bid you to come to use you for his glory. When he blesses you with a promotion at work, family restoration, healing, and in other ways, the process is overwhelming and wonderful. However, if you take your eyes off God, it's easy to lose sight of him as your source and begin to sink—like Peter. Instead of falling any further, stop and refocus on the Lord.

Oswald Chambers said, "You must agree with God and stop being the intensively striving kind of Christian you have been."[4] Pausing will help regain your focus on God, the One we should keep our eyes on. Whose voice will you answer? Agree with God that you will do things his way and not yours. It is necessary to answer his call and stop, think, and listen to his instructions as you walk the journey in faith.

Reflection: Today, what can you streamline to answer the call, regain sight of the Father, and give less attention to the storm around you?

Prayer: Father, I desire to align my life with your will. I humbly yield my heart in agreement with you. I appreciate your strength in times of weakness. Keep my gaze on you. Amen.

5

TRAINING FOR THE GOLD

Whoever gives heed to instruction prospers,
and blessed is the one who trusts in the Lord.

PROVERBS 16:20

LIKE MANY OF YOU, I grew up captivated by the Olympic Games, marveling at the athletes' precision, form, timing, and accuracy of execution in their events. As I matured, I saw the parallels between their discipline and dedication and the Christian practices for spiritual development. Athletes and Christians require faith, focus, commitment, and guidance to accomplish the desired gold medal of victory. Their success criteria are nearly identical, for an athlete's training and maintenance routines are similar to the time and discipline Christians need for relationship building with God to pursue his goals in a competitive world. Throughout Olympic history, the importance of quality coaching, consistent hard work, and following instructions is evident in the lives of competitors. Their testimonies are consistent whether they win or lose—the importance of intentional hard work and focus.

Are you ready for a victorious public and private life? It will require discipline and dedication to obtain "God's Gold." The best Coach is ready to help if you make room in your schedule to form a relationship and get to know him better through daily prayer, Scripture reading, meditation, and other spiritual practices.

The necessary discipline to obtain advice from God involves slowing down long enough to submit a petition or ask questions, then patiently wait, listen, or watch for the answer. Athletes likewise commit to scheduling hours of morning, day, or evening training with their coach or trainer. During these times, they are given specific instructions in corrective action and skill-building techniques to qualify for the Olympic Games. Medal winners are almost always the ones who follow the instructions exactly.

Are you ready to win the gold? Let's start with the basics and build a foundation for maturing your relationship with God the Father by trusting his leading by faith rather than trusting in your skills, gifts, and talents alone. Some of you may have a strong foundation but have picked up some bad habits that have caused distance between you and God. What if an athlete relied solely on their gift alone? How successful would they become? How long would they last in the games? It is God's will for his children to prosper in life. This is accomplished by gleaning insight from the Bible and living obediently to God. You can live with sustainable victory and joy if you choose to work smarter, not harder, through quiet moments in the presence of God.

WISDOM IS BETTER THAN GOLD

Proverbs 16:16 states, "How much better to get wisdom than gold, to get insight rather than silver!" Athletes who do not train regularly or follow the rules risk being disqualified from events or stripped of their medals. How often as a Christian have you felt stripped, disqualified, or unqualified at work, home, school, or church? At the time of similar disappointments, what did you learn about the situation in private time with God?

There have been many times my focus on the spiritual was skewed and I got off track. It was mostly because I was trying to operate in my own strength and skillset. This can happen when we do one of the following:

- disobey God's voice of leading when in quiet time
- resist the voice of the Holy Spirit speaking through a person God sends our way
- refuse to take time to stop and get instructions for God's best in our life
- become spiritually off balance to the point of being unable to sense God's leading
- come up with excuses why we have felt stripped, a failure, or disappointed

To get to the gold, remember the importance of balanced living. God desires that we are prosperous in spirit, mind, and body. The Bible says about Hezekiah that "in everything that he undertook in the service of God's temple and in obedience to the law and the commands, he sought his God and worked wholeheartedly. And so he prospered" (2 Chronicles 31:21). Being aligned spiritually can lead to a healthy mind and encourage us to care for our bodies. Let's strengthen our spiritual relationship first and watch how everything will work for our good as we pursue the kingdom of God and his righteousness. We are on a journey that challenges us to seek out God in a new way.

You will have to give your whole heart, with no more fragmentation, time lag, or forgetting your appointments with God. In other words, no more compromise. Believe in yourself to win the gold with your Creator and real Life Coach. It will cost you, but I sense through God's presence that you are ready for a lasting change. In private time with God you will expand your vision and knowledge as you mature spiritually, if you are devoted to your spiritual and personal development. As Proverbs 2:3-5 promises:

> Indeed, if you call out for insight
>   and cry aloud for understanding,
> and if you look for it as for silver
>   and search for it as for hidden treasure,

then you will understand the fear of the LORD
and find the knowledge of God.

LEARNING FROM JESUS HOW TO SEEK GOD

Jesus was bi-vocational as the Son of God, with a ministry assignment and an early career as a blue-collar worker—a carpenter. This dual career life had to be tiresome, causing wear and tear on his human body. Like any of us, Jesus would get tired and need proper rest. Even after he was in full-time ministry, his life was filled with a full schedule: moving from place to place and teaching, preaching, healing the sick, feeding the hungry, and raising the dead. How and when did he have time for communion with the Father?

The Bible reveals that Jesus did nothing but only what his Father instructed him to do. This is an excellent way to stay on task and accomplish goals. We are reassured and confident when we follow Jesus' example in early morning moments of solitude, if we build our spiritual foundation on the promises of God's Word and make them part of our everyday lives. The only way to learn those promises is to spend time in activities like Bible reading, praying, and reflective journaling. You will discover a fresh expression of God's presence as you seek his counsel daily. This practice helps us discern and distinguish God's voice. Knowing God's voice prevents us from being led astray, helping us maintain our spiritual birthrights and closeness to God. Staying connected to God is the source of successful living and is associated with an abundant life far beyond material prosperity, worldly achievements, and accomplishments.

Jesus is the prime example of pursuing and achieving godly goals. He was focused on his earthly assignment, just as you and I are focused on our careers, ministries, and dreams. The difference is that Jesus never yielded to the pressures of Satan, the Jews, or the Romans to perform miracles or do other things to prove his identity, without the Father's leading. He let nothing prevent him from slowing down long enough to pause in prayer with his Father. He valued and honored the time spent in his human relationship with God.

JESUS PRESSED PAUSE

Let's scroll through the "social media" pages in the Gospels to see Jesus fulfilling his earthly assignments: ministering to the people, mentoring and preparing the disciples for his departure, and dealing with life issues like grief on hearing about the death of his earthly cousin John the Baptist. Yet he always found time to press pause to spend time alone with the Father God: "When Jesus heard what had happened, he withdrew by boat privately to a solitary place. Hearing of this, the crowds followed him on foot from the towns" (Matthew 14:13).

This passage shows us the effect of workload and the need for solitude for refreshing moments with God. We see Jesus at work in Matthew 13, teaching many people the theme of the kingdom of heaven in a cluster of seven parables along the shore of Galilee. Then, in Matthew 14, he deals with a personal crisis and shows compassion for the welfare of those who followed him to Nazareth. One would assume Jesus was tired.

As an adjunct professor, I have experienced overwhelming exhaustion in preparing, teaching, assessing, tutoring, and managing student expectations. This is probably how Jesus felt: depleted spiritually, mentally, and physically, as he wanted the listening multitude to understand the concept of the kingdom of heaven. The narrative reveals Jesus' compassion and teaches the necessity of balanced living by describing how Jesus shows the significance of integrated care for the body and spirit.

Mark's Gospel also integrates Jesus' need for rest, solitude, and prayer. This idea is first noted in Mark 1:35, "Very early in the morning, while it was still dark, Jesus got up, left the house and went off to a solitary place, where he prayed." The passage alludes to Jesus sleeping at night then waking up early in the morning; he leaves his bed and goes to a solitary place to pray.

A second account of Jesus pausing is Mark 6: 31-32: "Then, because so many people were coming and going that they did not even have a chance to eat, he said to them, 'Come with me by yourselves to a quiet place and get some rest.' So they went away by themselves in a boat to a solitary place."

Read the verses again and see these components in operation, considering how hard Jesus had worked as a servant leader caring for God's people. The need was never-ending as the people kept following Jesus and the disciples. The disciples' gifts and talents, and the anointing of God on Jesus, did not preclude them from or substitute for the required rest the human body needs, so he slowed down to replenish himself and the disciples and gain spiritual renewal for the next task.

The third account of Jesus pausing is in Mark 6:45-52, after Jesus feeds the five thousand.

> Immediately Jesus made his disciples get into the boat and go on ahead of him to Bethsaida. . . . After leaving them, he went up on a mountainside to pray.
>
> Later that night, the boat was in the middle of the lake, and he was alone on land. He saw the disciples straining at the oars, because the wind was against them. Shortly before dawn he went out to them, walking on the lake. He was about to pass by them, but when they saw him walking on the lake, they thought he was a ghost. They cried out, because they all saw him and were terrified.
>
> Immediately he spoke to them and said, "Take courage! It is I. Don't be afraid." Then he climbed into the boat with them, and the wind died down. They were completely amazed, for . . . their hearts were hardened.

What are your thoughts as you read this narrative? Jesus provides the disciples and himself with a break after serving the community. The symbolism is beautiful: Jesus gives an example of getting away from the noise—the disciples in the boat and himself on the mountain. How significant is the isolation in the mountain, praying secretly before engaging the community again? What comes to mind is that

Jesus found time for solitude with his Father, and it was significant. Before the time of separation, the following was considered:

1. Jesus knew everyone needed time to regroup and rest after a day's work.
2. The disciples were sent away in the boat to go to the other side of Bethsaida.
3. The crowd was sent away.
4. Jesus went to a solitary place on a mountain.

Mountains are places of height that give access to reflection, a broad view of the land's capacity, and mental and spiritual illumination in the presence of God. Can these types of "mountaintop" experiences happen anywhere we designate a pause space?

After Jesus prayed, he became aware of strategies for his next journey, the storm, and the disciples' disbelief (hardened hearts) as he gained access to God's presence. Next, we see that Jesus is on land alone, and the disciples are nearly midway through their travel on the water when he sees a storm brewing and the disciples begin fretting.

Jesus could have walked past and not revealed himself, but his divine insight and care led him to their rescue. It is unclear what the disciples were doing during their quiet time before the storm. I suggest they were not reflecting on the day's miracles, their leader and who he was, nor were they praying—because they did not recognize Jesus and feared until they heard his voice say "Take courage! It is I. Don't be afraid" (Mark 6:50). How intimately did they know Jesus? Their response seems to indicate a lack of intimacy with Jesus.

One would think that their relationship with Jesus would have evolved to knowing, trusting, honoring, and having confidence in him. But they had not matured spiritually, even though they had already spent significant time together in work and fellowship. Instead, the passage confirms the shallowness of their relationship with Jesus as he entered the boat, the wind miraculously ceased its threats, and the disciples sat wondering. Did they have the same thought pattern as many in their community, uncertainty about whether Jesus was truly the Messiah? Did they know him?

In his Gospel, the physician Luke describes Jesus taking a break after teaching another multitude of people at Lake Gennesaret, instructing professional fishermen how to cast their nets, and healing a man of leprosy. In Luke 5:16, he notes how Jesus departed into the wilderness to pray, rest, and commune with his Father after his work. The chapter continues with narratives of the busyness of Jesus' life, as he taught crowds of people who followed him, dealt with the Pharisees and lawyers, and performed a healing miracle on a man with palsy.

What is the critical point about Jesus' example of seeking God? The moments of slowing down refreshed the power of God in Jesus and enabled him to flow with full confidence in God. After spending time in the presence of the Father, Jesus demonstrated miracles with what reads like little effort. This is what favor looks like. Also, God's grace was upon Jesus, enabling him to accomplish every aspect of his earthly assignment.

Living without applying God's standards has short- and long-term consequences. Struggles, disappointments, failures, ups and downs can all become more manageable when we learn to include God in our daily plans and develop a relationship of support, guidance, and hope for successful living. For example, as a sixteen-year-old high school senior preparing for college, I dreamed of living in New Haven, Connecticut, making a life in the medical profession, and becoming a speaker and author. Even though I was also young in my faith walk, I knew I had to reach out to God in prayer and trust him. My grades and test scores were not top-notch, but I knew God had a plan for me. I did not know where the finances would come from, but I trusted him for the outcome. As David Jeremiah has said, "Don't let obstacles along the road to eternity shake your confidence in God's promises."[1]

Regardless of your age or how long you've been on your faith walk, make God a priority as Jesus did on earth . . . he is the best example of knowing when to pause. If you are moving with breakneck speed, you are unable to know what task to leave undone on your to-do list. It will certainly help if you identify the cause of your spiritual imbalance to correct poor time management habits. This will help you to better implement solutions for the condition(s) that are manifested in spiritual disconnection. What spiritual malady might you be suffering from?

HURRY SYNDROME

To this point, we have learned how Jesus taught discipline and the need to prioritize solitude and prayer to build a relationship with the Father. As disciples of Christ, we can follow his example of prioritizing solitude and prayer and become familiar with navigating through the action steps of pressing pause daily.

A good athletic coach knows that if a team member shows signs of impatience (a "hurry syndrome") or stubbornness, they will have difficulty being still, listening, observing, and learning the playbook for practice. Many people might have a hurry syndrome that leads to a form of hyperactivity, which is marked by an overscheduled life. They, like others, are living in a world of excess and mindless motion and have no boundaries or regard for the will of God in their life.

How would you classify your spiritual readiness concerning an agreement to morning prayer, Bible reading, and reflective journaling? Can you recognize in yourself one of these hurry syndromes?

- *Scuttle sickness.* When an individual slow walks or abandons plans. In this case, the person desires more intimacy with God and plans to rise early, pray, read, and do other things to nurture their relationship; however, they never honor their scheduled meeting with God. There is always a good excuse. This person doesn't see a benefit to time in his presence.

- *Fast fever.* Perhaps you view prayer, Bible reading, and reflective journaling as a chore to quickly check off daily, forgetting it is really a committed time of sitting in God's presence. On the go you often whisper a prayer saying, "God knows my heart." This would be diagnosed as "fast fever," an indication of no value or patience to make time for spiritual intimacy. This person's schedule has nearly every hour filled with what they think is vital on their projected timeline.

- *Frenzy sickness.* If you become easily frustrated, with an attitude, and have fiery sparks of anger, this is a significant symptom of hurry syndrome that I call "frenzy sickness." This individual is no longer sensitive to their spiritual needs and lacks insight into their emotional intelligence and God's compassion toward others.

- *Indecisive anomaly.* None of the above accurately describes your unreadiness to include time with God in your schedule. You are sensitive to the need for God but not sure when you will find time. You are convinced that you are not disciplined enough to schedule time to shelter in the presence of God.

The apostle Paul teaches the instructional value of learning Scripture as "useful for teaching, rebuking, correcting and training in righteousness, so that the servant of God may be thoroughly equipped for every good work" (2 Timothy 3:16-17). Let's remember what Jesus did and find a solution to incorporate time with God and his Word daily. This process will allow us to intimately pursue God's master plan and our life purpose with an individualized blueprint and regain control of our spiritual journey.

Training for the gold to flourish as a Christian is doable; pursuing our goals without God's plan is difficult. The struggle of pause is real, but possible to overcome with the right tools and guidance. Understanding the importance of implementing steps for spiritual growth training requires learning to balance life. The first step is to allow and submit to spiritual homeostasis to reset your life's pace and pivot toward abundant living. Discipline is a choice of behavior to build a framework to avoid distractions and sustain a commitment of an active covenant. Christian growth and development can be like an athlete's training for quality performance.

I pray that your trust in God will expand as you read this book. Let's be honest: The enemy, the spirit of darkness, doesn't want you to build your relationship with Jesus, the Light of the World, and will create distractions and hindrances. Don't believe the lies that you don't have time to pause, and "It doesn't take all that." Yes, it does, and more. Our team began praying for you, dear readers, while the book was being written, to block the obstacles you might face in starting to exercise pause. The obstacles may appear problematic, but no matter how high the blockade is stacked, it cannot compare to the might of God; he is bigger. It is up to you to press pause and move toward your gold. Keep in mind, "Now is the time to know that God is able. To connect your current reality with God's present ability."[2]

PAUSE ON PURPOSE 5

ACT NOW

*Faith by itself, if it is not accompanied
by action, is dead.* – JAMES 2:17

While sitting in a comfortable chair on my deck, reading my Bible and scrolling through a list of positive affirmations, I looked up into the sky as the sun's warmth massaged my face. It was a morning pause before launching into the rest of my day. It would be one day in a week of many moving parts, stressful decisions, and possibly sleepless nights.

At the core of my being, I asked the Lord what steps I should take. Silently I sat, waiting and listening for a sign—some impression that would provide courage and motivation to act as led by the Spirit. Nothing happened immediately, but as I paced the length of the deck and sat on the steps, breathing deeply, two words from John 16:33 crossed my mind: "Take heart." In other words, be courageous.

At the same time, my human logic and reasoning tried to take center stage in my mind. I thought about the budget deficit and other concerns related to upcoming events I was involved with, yet I continued to stay in pause mode, meditating on that same Scripture: "I have told you these things, so that in me you may have peace" (John 16:33).

I felt the weight of the burden become lighter as I focused on thanking God for knowing days like this would come for all his followers and having his Word in place as a guide for Christians to access. At that time, John 16:33 encouraged me to follow the team's plan and to place my concerns in the Lord's hands. I believed God could answer prayer, but how would he answer my prayer this time?

When in the valley of pressing issues and critical decisions, pausing on purpose can redirect your focus to God's power to overcome any Goliath that tries to keep you paralyzed in fear and doubt. It can also reassure you that when your works are coupled with faith, plans can be executed with a guarantee of triumphant results that glorify God.

The application of pause proves that it is worthwhile to train for God's gold with Bible study, prayer each day for guidance, and endurance to pursue dreams, goals, and other assignments in the confidence that he is near.

Reflection: Do multiple tasks on your schedule prevent you from being obedient in moments of pause with the Lord? What are they? What are you hesitating about? How can you take action by faith now?

Prayer: Father, I desire to turn my affection toward you, serve you, and be successful in my life's call. Help me choose what is essential to make room in my day for you and become who you designed me to be as I pause to read, listen to you, and obey. Amen.

6

PAUSE FOR MORE OF GOD

Be still, and know that I am God.

PSALM 46:10

STORMS CAN BE FRIGHTENING. Especially when an electrical flash of lightning pierces through the room, followed by the loud noise of thunder. Momma would say, "It's a storm. Turn off the lights, come into the living room, and sit still while God does his work." She would turn off the TV, right in the middle of our favorite show. Or if we were dancing in the family room to the stereo, she would lift the handle off the vinyl record, nearly scratching it with the swift motion of the needle gliding across it, before turning it off as well.

Sitting still in the darkness with all lights out, rain hitting the windows, and lightning and thunder continuing, we listened to one another breathe until the storm was over. Even if we nodded off and fell asleep, she would wake us up because the Lord was at work (and we didn't need to miss what he was doing). This true story is rooted in the fact that my mom was raised in the country (some call it the *Deep South*), where they experienced severe coastal storms. Explanations for these events included a mixture of folklore, superstition, and the Bible. Her theology of God was filled with fear and trauma, as reflected in how she quieted and gathered her children in stillness during a storm. However, the lessons observed and learned from her example transcend fear: Beyond any potential danger or trauma, my mother taught another way to reverence the work of God's hands and his presence—the importance of remaining attentive and maintaining alertness, stillness, and watchfulness, and to listen even during the storm.

This life story can help us learn and understand what can occur when we pause in stillness. We can draw closer to God as faith increases and as we learn to distinguish God's voice and recognize him at work through various seasons and storms. We must model Christ in a world with so many distractive "gods" that we can so easily fall into spending time with. God is always available to us, but when we make ourselves more available to him, access to him is better. Our goal and desire should be to pause daily and seek him first, not for what we can get, but because we have learned to love and trust him. Embracing more of God evolves as we see the need to invest in our spiritual health and begin to see the vastness of God's presence in home life, work, and life in general.

Scripture is a type of injunction from God. In law, there are three types of injunctions: permanent, temporary, or preliminary. An injunction is a restraining order to do or cease doing a specific action. How is God attempting to restrain you from doing or ceasing doing a particular action, in order to gain your attention? Psalm 46:10-11 reveals God's passion for us to stop whatever else we are doing, to exalt him above all the other things on the earth, and to acknowledge his presence with us. "He says, 'Be still, and know that I am God; I will be exalted among the nations, I will be exalted in the earth.' The LORD Almighty is with us; the God of Jacob is our fortress."

In this passage, let's look at God differently—as a judge. Verse 10 opens with an injunction: "Be still." This passage's injunction is as strong as when Jesus commanded the storm to cease. In other words, hear him giving the order to "Press pause in what you are doing today and give me the glory above all else." Regular, ongoing pause times are like a permanent injunction and can create permanent change in our lives. The time of stillness before and after an activity, like a temporary injunction, honors the presence of God and reinforces intimacy and confidence in trusting him to fulfill his Word.

These verses should invoke an urgency to respond as we learn that he is our refuge. Psalm 46 states this clearly in the first verse and proceeds to say that this is the case no matter what happens, regardless of the situation. Even when the children of Israel were shaken, they were reminded to be full of confidence because God had intervened in wars and other adverse situations before, and he would do it again because he honors covenant relationships.

During turbulent times at home or work, taking a moment to be still results in clarity of thought, guidance with solutions, and peace that God is Lord over all things on earth. This confidence comes from learning to pause and know him in prayer, reading, and seeing him at work in every situation. Quiet time develops faith, acquaints us with God's voice, helps us mature our spiritual image of God, and gives us the confidence to face the noise of thunder after following his guidance. It also allows God to be involved in our daily lives, giving us singleness of mind as our souls and physical bodies prosper in health.

STILL WATERS RUN DEEP

The room was filled with groups of people talking, background noise from the band, and clusters of table talk conversations as the servers weaved in and out with trays of drinks and food samples while waiting for the reception to begin. Watching the various tables, I thought about how the noise level interrupted intimate conversations, limiting the ability to identify individual voices. When a server accidentally dropped a tray of drinks, it crashed loudly on the floor and caused a temporary pause of silence from everyone in the room (except the band).

Storms come, whether they are angry voices in meetings at work, crises in our homes, or other undesirable situations. They clamor to block our consciousness of hope and dependence on our relationship with God. In my life journey, I went through a period when my medical practice began to thrive. And then I was diagnosed with cancer, and our teenage children began to explore life independently of God.

This is when I learned that "still waters run deep." Already having the practice and discipline of quiet time, I had to lean in even more. Many times, I lay prostrate on the floor, smelling the carpet, staying in my literal prayer closet in the house with my Bible and journal, praying and listening. There, I embraced stillness while it seemed the world was caving in on me. I chose to pause in contemplation as to my next steps.

Our human mindset toward relationship building is often complex, especially regarding a relationship with an invisible God. Society has created many available substitutes to occupy our time and can deceive us into thinking that pausing to sit and read the Bible is an ineffective waste of time. The phrase "still waters run deep" is accurate when we practice pause. In the stillness, we identify God at work in our life more as a child of a rich spiritual heritage. Spiritually healthy individuals can more securely sustain the storms of life by knowing they are in harmony with God's plan for their lives. Stillness, although complex in a fluid world, enables the believer to look through the lens of God's original design for humanity for fruitfulness in all things, reproducing the life of Christ on the earth.

Living in the fast lane with no time for God is like being in the rapid whitewater of the Ocoee River near Chattanooga, Tennessee, where our church couples ministry would go whitewater rafting. The beauty of the blustering water glistened as we swiveled and turned, screaming with laughter. Once, we were on the lake, moving so fast that one of the passengers was not secured and flipped out into the water. When he fell into the water, the guide and the others were telling him to swim from under the raft, but he could not hear because of the sound of the water. You could see his hand pounding on the bottom from underneath the raft, and we wished it had a hidden trap door we could open to help him. When he stopped panicking, he finally heard us saying "Swim from under," and his face had a much calmer expression. He trusted the guide and did what he said: Take hold of the oars, stand up, and we will pull you into safety.

Think about a time when you were so busy with your concerns that an unexpected stressful situation came your way. Because you were unprepared or unable to deal with it, you may have started swirling in the chaos until you hit a situational hole that added to the turmoil, and you became deaf to the voice of God in a total state of confusion. You can only calm down long enough to regain perspective and seek guidance through turbulence when you separate yourself from it. A place of stillness is necessary and required for refreshing the mind.

God has often allowed challenging issues to come into my life with a shattering noise that causes me to stop everything on my journey of purpose. Yes, I silence my activities and redirect my attention toward him. Have you ever become ill all of a sudden and had to put everything you thought necessary on hold? What about a family crisis? Interestingly, these eye-openers typically remove the excessive noise of other voices long enough for us to hear God's voice and understand what he has been saying and trying to show us for a long time. In moments like these, I realize in hindsight that I often saw the signs and heard his voice, but had so many other distractions that I thought those were "echoes in the wind." I thought the signs were trying to prevent the progress in life and did not recognize God's calling to pause to hear him.

It was when I was lying in bed during nearly two years of chemotherapy that I wondered what I had missed. I loved people, served the church, community, and family, and prayed and read the Bible. My mind reflected on a distant hunger for time alone with God in genuine prayer, reading, praise, and worship for an hour or more. Those were refreshing times: Work and servanthood were manageable, faith was easily activated. There was nothing that I would not entrust to God to handle, because I trusted our relationship. It was easy to hear his leading, and the result was favorable when I obeyed his voice.

There were times before the diagnosis when I was so busy that I fell asleep with my Bible and woke up late, rushing out the door. It was a rush, with diminished quality time for God. This led to a life of spiritual dryness, as if in a desert. There was no fresh creativity, revelation, or direct acquaintance with God. Who left the relationship? I did not realize that my "ego" (edging God out) affected my daily life.

Learning to take purposeful pauses throughout the day assured my understanding of the instructions for my destiny according to God's plans and purposes. In the stillness between meetings, patients, and phone calls, there was a sense of his presence and a desire to bow in reflective Scripture and worship. In faith, this fellowship with him prompted the discovery of direction for the next steps that day. How often do you stop in your day in thanksgiving for what has been accomplished with his grace and help?

Genesis 2:2-3 says, "And on the seventh day God ended his work which he had made; and he rested on the seventh day from all his work which he had made. And God blessed the seventh day and sanctified it: because that in it he had rested from all his work which God created and made" (KJV). God is a perfect example of getting still and resting after completing a six-day task. He blessed it as the first Sabbath—a day of rest. On this spiritual journey, we don't have to wait until Sunday worship service, but we can get still anywhere or at any time in his presence to become refreshed for strength and illumination for the next step toward purpose. We don't have to wait for thunderstorms or life crises of faith to seek God's assistance. Stillness refreshes our outlook and overall perspective throughout life, day by day. There is joy, hope, and strategic wisdom to limit striving in our strength because we have a Father who cares about all that concerns us.

SPIRITUAL HERITAGE OF GOD'S CHILDREN

The practice of pressing pause daily assures us that we can stop and disconnect from the world's way and plug into him for anything. Looking through the lens of God's original design for humanity, there is a promise of fruitfulness in all things as we reproduce a life of Christlikeness on the earth.

Healthy interpersonal relationships help us understand our spiritual heritage and ascertain the promises for successful living. In Ephesians 2:11-22, Paul clearly shows the challenge between the Gentiles and the Jews in response to Jesus and his availability to all humanity. There was a shortage of unity and peace among them about who had access to the promise as children of God. The Gentiles succumbed to feeling inferior, in contrast to the Jews, who expressed an unhealthy image of superiority as the chosen ones. Let's look at how Paul describes peace as the solution to disunity.

The solution to disunity is found in the understanding that God sent Jesus to rid the divide between Jews and Gentiles, making salvation (abundant living) available to all who believe. Paul's letter makes clear that regardless of one's birth family, circumcised or not, God's promise is available to everyone. There are many divisions in our world, creating the "haves" and the "have nots"; even in the church, there are those who appear to be super-spiritual, those who are unsure of their position with God, and those who haven't had time for God and lost hope in his availability to them. As Paul taught, no one is inferior or superior in his eyes. Anyone and all who accept his Son and are obedient to his Word have access to eternal life and the promises of God through our intimacy with him.

Learning to pause with God in his presence is the source of relationship building with the Father. God is not found in Google searches, AI use, or social media scrolls, but in actual time with him. The lost art of prayer, Bible reading, and journaling has been forgotten in an attempt to keep up with society's pace. But in time with God, we become better prepared to handle life as we trust and follow the Holy Spirit's guiding voice through the many cares that can swallow us up in the storms of life.

Whether natural, situational, mental, or emotional, storms will come and disrupt our peace. The interruption to peace builds barriers of disharmony in spirit, mind, and body. Each component has a need that seeks peace in various ways. Remembering to hesitate in the rhythms of our life forms space for finding insight to sustain our peace amid storms. During my spiritual growth, I found that when my peace was disturbed, my decision-making was not the best, and I was not the best to hang out with emotionally. A pastoral staff member at my home church, always reminded me, "Go back and get your peace wherever you left it." In other words, I needed to return to my behavioral state before internal chaos bombarded my quietness with God. I needed to gain his help in managing my present state of being.

The act of solitude is mocked and deemed unnecessary, but those who sincerely devote themselves to enrichment in Scripture can see how God sees them and live accordingly, being productive and producing lasting fruit. Kindness, gentleness, love, long-suffering, and the other fruit of the Spirit will reveal the expressed image of God and provoke others to ask how they can know him. The impact of God-seekers on the earth will be visible, reproducing the likeness of Jesus. They will find the strength to accomplish their goals and dreams and endure life with peace and joy.

We live in a world of many barriers that have divided our time with God (even including many useful activities and opportunities). The longer we divide our time, the more doubt can creep in and increase, unless we include spiritual maintenance to strengthen our awareness of God. Modern living requires scheduling time for spiritual balance, which is the primary source of recognizing the power of the Holy Spirit in everyday life.

This covenant relationship with the Father includes the give-and-take of spending time with him and accepting his leadings and blessings for our lives. Understanding the value of this time in God's presence is vital to stabilizing faith, knowing his voice, and living with a righteous conscience that empowers us to live in ways that exemplify Christ's likeness. In time, confidence replaces doubt that the Holy

Spirit is unreliable like humans. The more we seek his presence, the more we will embrace his character, quickly recognizing the Holy Spirit under any circumstance to live fruitfully.

FACE-TO-FACE

The dilemma in understanding one's personal relationship with God is not unusual, especially when so many religions exist that state that their way is the way (or one of many ways) to God. It is essential to return to Bible study, quiet time, and weekly worship to strengthen our knowledge of the Word and discern truth from false teachings that further divert the attention of so many. There is only one way to God: through a personal relationship with Jesus Christ.

Staying connected in any family is important, and as children of God, Christians have a Father. It is essential to remain connected to the Father through the presence of the Holy Spirit. We stay connected by communication. The more we engage with God, the more we recognize and submit to his presence. Since the Covid-19 pandemic, we have lived in a virtual era of Zoom, Teams, and more ways to connect and communicate. We are made aware of scheduled meetings and can exercise options to virtually "show up," even if we ignore the video and turn on mute.

My point is that our busyness becomes an excuse to do the same thing spiritually—not being fully engaged or committed when we do try to commune with him. Look at your calendar—how much time is allocated to God? The Hebrew word for *presence* is commonly translated as "face," implying a personal encounter (Exodus 33:11; Deuteronomy 34:10). In this book, *presence* should be considered a face-to-face personal encounter with God through the Holy Spirit. The presence of God is wherever you choose to approach him. In that space of encounter, your coooperation and commitment to engage are necessary.

To attain more of anything worth reaching for, you must approach and get as close as possible—right in the face of the item. There is no comparison between a virtual conversation and a face-to-face conversation with someone you are attempting to know or grow in relationship with. A spiritually healthy relationship requires us to get in the face of God and hold close to his very essence.

Uninterrupted intimacy with the Lord is a space for developing spirit and mind as we read and listen to the Spirit teach and guide our life. Understanding the wealth of wisdom and knowledge that is attainable via a consistent relationship with God empowers us to work smarter, not harder. Face-to-face daily time with God minimizes stress, worry, and disease processes in our bodies because we will better care for ourselves. Beginning our day with God is crucial in developing and focusing on spiritual homeostasis to become spiritually healthy and to function optimally.

When researching self-help modalities for making transformative changes, the consumer often disregards the topic of seeking more of God. Since you are reading this book, you must have considered God's guidance as a means of self-help and personal development. Prioritizing your day is pivotal to how balanced your day will be—clear and concise, or haphazard and unorganized? Knowing what to say no or yes to aids in scheduling purposeful tasks and activities for your life.

Pausing to prioritize time with God is the compass of goal fulfillment. The idea of success in our home, work, relationships, or business is a sense of peace and happiness. Sure, we want to be financially comfortable; however, money without peace and joy is an additional hurdle to achieving and enjoying life goals. The promise of abundant life is much more than a life of fame and fortune. Investment in spiritual health is a definite modality for a healthy spirit, mind, and body when the Scripture is implemented with balanced living. Dare to grow closer to God each day and watch him awaken you morning by morning with new mercy, joy, and strength to accomplish tasks to complete your daily journey. Pausing in the morning and throughout the day is a type of time out, a pit stop for face-to-face rejuvenation, to be redirected and readjusted by the Master Planner of the blueprint for our lives.

Isaiah 50:4 teaches that God gives us the words we must say during home, work, and business decision-making. He is the source of coaching for any vocation: "The Sovereign LORD has given me a well-instructed tongue, to know the word that sustains the weary. He wakens me morning by morning, wakens my ear to listen like one being instructed." This passage discloses the challenges of suffering as a byproduct of being a believer in God, while still trusting and believing in his availability to help us through any situation. Isaiah gives words to bring hope, sustainability, and direction for himself and the people because of spending time with the Lord to lead and guide others.

Like the Israelites, we find ourselves in dilemmas that require access to wisdom, knowledge, encouragement, and strength to sustain ourselves through life's storms in the valley of our decisions. In this Scripture, one should understand that God has a word for the weary listener in his presence. Are you weary? Are you tired of the "rat race" of life? The Scriptures invite you to pause and receive its words for renewed faith and strength.

More stillness with God builds a relationship with him and provides believers with a better understanding of the nuanced values in his dealings with us. When the children of God were taken away from their homeland into years of captivity and bondage, they had to stay focused on the Scriptures to remember and trust in the promises of their God for deliverance. Life was difficult, but they survived by standing on the Word of God taught to them through generations. Today our world is experiencing various forms of difficulty; however, we must move forward each day with focus and purpose, assured that God will fulfill his end of the covenant relationship as we do our part to seek him. How do we do this? Press pause in reading, reflective listening, communicative prayer, and recitation of Scriptures.

The essential need for "time in God's face" is that it allows us to be spiritually fit to disarm the invisible enemy's attacks, which manifest in many ways in our daily lives. The children of Israel were distracted in a different way than we are today, captive for seventy years in Babylon and stripped of the familiar routines of worship. Remember, only the most skilled and talented were selected and taken into captivity. They were probably like many we know today: competitive, focus-driven, with Type A personalities, obsessed with the desire for success and innovation in a new setting, with fewer restrictions on obedience. The Israelites had to learn to improvise for survival, while continuing to reverence God by pausing to press in daily to keep the Word of God in their hearts.

In today's world, we likewise find ourselves in various levels of captivity to the ways of this society, with many being pressured to pursue worldly accolades, promotions, fame, or fortune. Distracted from the call to rest in God's presence with overloaded schedules, our current lifestyles far too often destabilize our spiritual homeostasis, dull our taste buds for the things of God, and distance us from his affection and covenant relationship.

DO YOU WANT M.O.R.E.?

Jeremiah 29:13 says, "You will seek me and find me when you seek me with all your heart." We will become disciplined as we engage in God's presence in quiet time. That is the only way to have more of God in our life. What does it mean to experience M.O.R.E.? It stands for "Moving in Obedience Regardless of the Evidence," an acronym I heard years ago during a revival at my home church.

You might be saying, "Yes, I want more. What does it cost?" It costs action and faith. That is what it takes to begin the discipline of pausing. Sometimes, your quiet time will be filled with praise and worship. At other times, you will feel rushed, distracted, or solemn. No matter how you feel, the bottom line is to be consistent and have a sincere heart to please God as you obey his Word.

Your validation of the importance of prioritizing time with God will further ignite your pursuit of godly living through quiet time. If you love God and desire to please him, you will learn to seek him before seeking man's counsel. You will enjoy meditating on his Word and be determined to walk holy and upright before humankind. When you "hunger and thirst for righteousness" (Matthew 5:6), you will seek to please and obey him regardless of your situation.

The Bible says in Lamentations 3:25-26, "The LORD is good to those who wait for Him, to the soul who seeks Him. It is good that one should hope and wait quietly for the salvation of the LORD" (NKJV). Develop a deeper relationship with the Lord. As you walk by faith, be strengthened in the joy of your salvation until he demonstrates his love toward you. Apply the principles of quiet time and be blessed. Growing spiritually not only helps you to trust God more fully, but it releases fresh faith that is able to move mountains.

PRIORITIZING TIME WITH GOD

If you feel distant from God, things don't have to stay that way. Yes, you can make a change and experience intimacy with him.

If you need to mend your relationship with the Father, don't delay. First, repent of all your sins. Apologize for not spending time in God's presence. Do not try to make any excuses for your choices and behaviors. If you have been lazy, acknowledge that. You must be honest, repentant, and ready to turn away from the ungodly thoughts, words, and behaviors that have kept you from making time for God. The good news is that God is ready to forgive you, and once you have accepted his forgiveness, you will desire to learn more about the character of such a merciful God. You also will have a greater desire to build your relationship with him in quiet time.

Second, once you have committed to turn away from your past behavior, decide to make time for God. Your eagerness for God's presence will increase as you begin to read the Scriptures and pray in your personal time with him. Remember, the foundation of your relationship will be strengthened as you consistently pray and search the Scriptures for guidance regarding your daily activities.

During quiet time, God will provide peace until specific instructions for your concerns are revealed. An idea can be conceived in prayer as the visitation of the Holy Spirit rests on you. There will be moments in prayer when you will receive insight to design the perfect plan for you to attain your goals. God provides all of this and more when you honor him.

Prioritizing time to honor God lays a foundation for moving into the rest of your day with a mind and heart open to God's leading. If your ears are attuned to the voice of God, it serves as a shield against the many other competing voices you encounter throughout the day. Having clarity of mind is a benefit of stillness in solitude. It is in this place of calm that you can let go and release control of your life to God.

PAUSE ON PURPOSE 6

LET GO

A time to search and a time to give up,
a time to keep and a time to throw away. — ECCLESIASTES 3:6

It isn't easy to let go of something we birthed or built from the ground up, or to let go of relationships or the power of a long-awaited position. There is no question that a sweet sense of pride and honor is felt when we have attained the goal we have worked hard for. Learning how to let go can be the hardest thing to do if we have given control of our life to this dream come true. Relinquishing what controls personal drive is difficult when one forgets the source and provider of their achievements. The supreme vision caster has been replaced and no longer sits on the throne of their heart.

In other words, the struggle comes when God no longer has first place. In Exodus 20:3, we are told to have no other God. The formation of an idol in our lives can occur so quickly and unnoticed, primarily when affection is segmented into chasing dreams, ideas, and visions that don't include God.

There was a time when I was working and seemingly productive in many organizations and ministries. Over a period of time, an emptiness overshadowed me. There was no joy in what I was doing, although what I did for God was good. I knew my time of being spread thin was coming to an end. But self-talk convinced me that I had to stay on board. I was exhausted, but still I would not surrender. Lack of regular time with God decreased my self-control to let go of having control. One day in prayer, I fell asleep, and awakened with a desire to resign from several positions. I realized that I was not in the perfect will of God but his permissive will.

Once I regained perspective and prioritized God first in my life in morning reading and prayer, I understood why it was so hard to let go of control: what I was doing was good, people were being helped, and provisions were being made to continue the work. But my time was up. Like Deuteronomy 6:12 says, "Be careful that you do not forget the Lord."

Reflection: When we keep God first, our hearts remain open to the leading of God. Setting priority for pause keeps our heart sensitive to God's voice. What or who is on the throne of your heart leading your life?

Prayer: Lord, I accept the call to live a life worthy of your calling. Help me prioritize my day as I seek you first for your perfect will to serve humanity and fulfill your purpose for my life.

Part 2

THE WHY FOR SPIRITUAL INTIMACY

*Maybe sometimes it's good to give up,
and surrender, lay still and wait . . . for God.*

LILIANA KOHANN

7

MEAL TIME
Have You Lost Your Appetite?

Taste and see that the LORD is good.

PSALM 34:8

||

A HEALTHY SPIRITUAL DIET is essential for maintaining spiritual homeostasis. Healthy, consistent portions of God's Word will increase our faith, trust, and strength and promote a healthy appetite for more of God's goodness. Practicing pause guides us into spiritual exercise, which aids in maintaining balance in life. The staple nutrients for spiritually balanced living are Scripture reading, reflection, and prayer to keep us aligned with the Father God as his children.

Is your appetite fulfilling God's will for your life? Knowing what is stealing your time and keeping you from spending direct time with God and personal self-care is essential to balanced and abundant living. Evaluating your spiritual meal plan reveals what controls your private and public cravings. What you consume energizes or weakens your spiritual lifestyle and impacts your priorities, mindset, and how you care for your body.

This chapter provides nourishment for our spiritual taste buds to experience the sweet and sour, feed on faith, and starve doubt. Our taste for God's goodness is developed by experiencing private time with him.

Pressing pause with God prevents us from nibbling on "fad diets" that will not sustain us during crises of faith, work-related issues, and home life. A religious fad diet consists of ideologies that allow for the compromise of God's covenant with humanity. It may open us up to the "it doesn't take all that" virus, giving us permission in the twenty-first century to negate parts of the Scriptures and dull our spiritual senses in obeying God. Typically, we begin to do much less corporate worship, private Bible reading, and prayer, and begin to crave satisfaction from cultural motivational quotes and positive affirmation. Before we know it, the hunger and thirst for righteousness is gone, and an acquired taste of offense lingers.

We cannot survive on these new spiritual fad diets. A planner filled with business activities or dinner meetings leaves no time for God and is not a sufficient meal. Matthew 4:4 reminds us: "Man shall not live on bread alone, but on every word that comes from the mouth of God." Discern what your palate has developed a taste for. It might be the item that is preventing you from pausing with God.

The tongue is a small structure in the body but has a major role in the digestive system and the functionality of what we choose to eat once we have tasted an item and enjoyed it. Our taste buds manage our cravings in many ways, sometimes leading to insufficient food selection for our health. Taste buds can become damaged by chemotherapy, medication, and physical injuries, in many cases eliminating the ability to savor once delectable food items.

Taste disorders indicate major changes and problems with our sense of taste. Have you ever had a bad cold and could not taste your favorite food? What about hot beverage drinkers (like me) who can take a sip too quickly and burn our tongue? Physiologically, as we age our sense of taste can be diminished. But spiritually, as we pause and mature, our desire to taste God's goodness increases. The more our relationship grows, the more our passion for delightful solitude with the Father increases. I like to say, "Take caution when taste-testing life choices. You don't want to ruin your appetite for the Bread of Life."

TASTE DISORDERS

There are parallel taste disorders in our physical and spiritual lives, as seen in table 7.1. A person with no room for God in their schedule is in the spiritual condition of *ageusia*, a total loss of desire for the things of God. As Psalm 10:4 reveals, "In his pride, the wicked man does not seek him; in all his thoughts there is no room for God."

Table 7.1. Natural versus spiritual sense of diminished taste

Natural Taste Disorders	Spiritual Taste Disorders
Natural Sense of Diminished Taste	*Spiritual Sense of Diminished Taste*
Ageusia: A complete loss of taste.	**Ageusia:** No desire or sense of urgency for God. (Ps 10:4)
Dysgeusia: Sense of taste is distorted.	**Dysgeusia:** A sense of compromise with good/evil. (Rom 12:9)
Hypergeusia: Sense of taste is heightened.	**Hypergeusia:** Super spiritual without fruit. (2 Tim 3:5)
Hypogeusia: Limited/reduced sense of taste.	**Hypogeusia:** Diminished passion for the life of godliness. (Prov 29.1)
Phantom taste: A lingering unpleasant taste.	**Phantom taste:** A lingering sense of offense. (Ps 119:165)

Individuals who compromise regarding their relationship with God have an appetite that waxes and wanes for God's love and the world's offerings. The tongue disorder of compromise is *dysgeusia*. A relationship with sincerity to please him enables us to be stable in our choices. We will make errors from time to time, but an all-out compromise results in our relationship with God being insincere. Our "love must be sincere. Hate what is evil; cling to what is good," warns Romans 12:9. This is a verse to live by when preserving an appetite for God's Word.

Those who have tasted of God's goodness and have fallen away are characterized by the tongue disorder *hypogeusia*. This is a person with a diminished passion for a life of godliness, becoming malnourished spiritually and having nearly no sense of God's presence in their life. They become stubborn and focused on their own idea of what is best. The Bible warns, "Whoever remains stiff-necked after many rebukes will suddenly be destroyed—without remedy" (Proverbs 29:1).

The more someone ignores time with God, the more an attitude of offense stirs, enlarging the gap between themselves and God. The symptoms of the next tongue disorder could be the result of church trauma, where some action by a church hurts an individual, and the sting of the impact inhibits a relationship with God or those who profess Christianity. This is known as the *phantom taste disorder*, with symptoms marked by nursing a memory of an offensive pain that lingers so strongly that it is felt as if it is happening over and over. This disorder stifles the expression of kindness to others. Offense retained in our hearts further deepens and accelerates deception, widening the gap between us and God.

There is also phantom disorder burnout of the taste for servanthood by a Christian who has not learned to pause their works and service for solitude. The enemy doesn't want the body of Christ to protect our relationship and obedience to the Word of God. We need to remain vigilant because our adversary is on the hunt for people of faith, using distractions to make one vulnerable to the attacks of Satan. Others become offended when they feel they have sacrificed more than others (not considering the sacrifice of the Father through Jesus) and have not been rewarded.

Moments in pause assist us in maintaining and regaining perspective. Pause protects us from losing sight of our purpose at home, work, and church. There is great peace when we submit to stillness in pause to obey God's Word: "Great peace have those who love your law, and nothing can make them stumble" (Psalm 119:165). Strength for endurance and avoidance of these taste disorders are some of the benefits of face-to-face time in God's presence.

HOW TO DISCRIMINATE THE TASTE
OF GOD'S GOODNESS

You are given a bowl with a white granular substance. It looks like salt, but is it sugar? Our world has so much to offer that can be distracting that we find ourselves tasting a little of everything to discover what we are being offered, and we fear being left out of the know.

Discerning God and his will for our lives doesn't require us to try the ways of the culture. We have been given an open-book test. If we read, pray, and reflect, we will be enlightened to the life of righteousness as a Christian. Like the experiential bowl with the white mixture mentioned above, we must taste the substance to differentiate between the item being salt or sugar.

The condiments salt and sugar have benefits; however, one is better than the other, depending on the need. Society offers many self-help methods, but the primary standard of care for humanity's needs is found in the Bible. How do we attain the knowledge, wisdom, and insight for daily living as children of God to impact our personal lives and communities? It begins with a personal pause in private time with God for the public victories in home, work, and community. The Scriptures are the guideline for a godly lifestyle—a moral compass.

Breaks from motion with the world to pause with God reveal a mirror image of who we should imitate—an authentic God of mercy and love. Sometimes, it is hard to distinguish a Christian from a non-Christian, like a wolf dressed in sheep's clothing. The character of God is visible in his children, and it becomes easy to know them by their fruit as we begin to study the Bible. Our society can identify those who live Christlike in every facet of their lives only by the consistent example they model. To begin modeling Christlikeness, one must recognize the positive or negative influences that feed or steal our time for a growing relationship of faith, and address the need to starve doubt and remove confusion to live effectively as a healthy Christian. It takes faith to become disciplined to press pause with God in a lifelong relationship of reading the Bible (tasting of

God's Word), prayer (communication with God), and reflection and journaling (meditation on Scripture and what has been impressed in your heart).

The seat at the covenant table is essential for meals for healthy spirituality, emotional stability, and physical stamina for purposeful living. Reading a balanced diet of Scripture will increase moral living as a revival of Scripture reading occurs in the land.

The trend of reading the Bible publicly and at home has changed. Sure, we use electronic devices for convenience, but don't forget the physical Bible—the actual turning of pages of the Bible has such an effect on the reader that it cannot be replaced with devices. Pause in the Scriptures is what synchronizes alignment with purpose designed specifically by God. When you press pause at the feet of God, his presence is the self-improvement for every accomplishment you are pursuing.

Consumption of a proper spiritual diet clarifies one's focus on how to journey through everyday life, crises of faith, and decision-making. Pause confirms Jesus' words: "Man shall not live on bread alone, but on every word that comes from the mouth of God" (Matthew 4:4). Naturally speaking, bread is not enough to live off, but it is filling. When we have protein, vegetables, and other food items, it ensures a balanced meal. Jesus, the all-sufficient One, informs us of the necessity of God's Word to be sustained. If you are living day to day without incorporating God into your schedule, imagine how much more effective you would be if you press pause in stillness with the Master Planner.

If you have not had time with God lately, don't let the guilt prevent you from returning to the table with God. He is waiting for you. Let's pause momentarily and ask forgiveness for our dismissive behavior of time with God: *Lord, forgive me for my lack of sensitivity and missing our time together, ignoring our relationship's health, denying my spirit your presence and your grace for strength to live a godly life. Father, I am returning to the table to be filled with life-giving wisdom to be sustained in this world.*

AWOL APPETITE?

Have you ever had a taste for a delicious dessert? Perhaps you had a longing for a special outfit, a new house, a new car, or jewelry. Your passion propelled you to pursue the thing that would satisfy your desire. You were willing to discipline yourself to do what it would take to attain the desire.

With respect to your relationship with the Lord, have you forgotten the discipline required for spiritual growth and development? Have you lost your appetite for the things of God? Have you lost the discipline to pursue him? If so, are you willing to make the necessary sacrifices to regain your spiritual appetite so you can restore or deepen your relationship with God? Think about how excited Christians are who have recently accepted salvation. They're on fire for God and full of zeal. They try to attend every church service, work night and day on committees planning activities for their church, and find time to daily pray and study the Bible.

They are true God-chasers, but over time, it seems their appetite for fellowship with God decreases. This happens to many believers for various reasons, but the most typical reason is schedule overload. Even too many church activities can contribute to a decline in spiritual zeal, which leads to spending less time with Father God. Please do not misunderstand me. It is good to serve in the local church; however, one must remember to personally seek first the kingdom of God and his righteousness (Matthew 6:33).

Perhaps your schedule is not the problem, but you still have not decided to pencil in time with God. Maybe spending time in prayer and Bible study just doesn't excite you enough to be on the top of your list of priorities. Certain characteristics manifest when believers lose their hunger and thirst for righteousness over time: they spend less time in corporate fellowship in church, personal prayers get shorter, they spend less time praising and worshiping God, and there's a dramatic decline in their Scripture reading.

We all experience spiritual highs and lows. The danger is when we neglect allocating time for God—our passion for Christ diminishes until we become spiritually depleted. Just as not eating food will cause our body to weaken, so not feeding our spirit through prayer, Bible study, and fellowship will make us spiritually weak. When we neglect quiet time, our soul no longer pants after God as the deer pants for water (Psalm 42:1). It is a dangerous thing when our appetite for intimacy with the Father decreases to nonexistence. When that happens, God's covenant promises are distant from our lives: "Remember that at that time you were separate from Christ, excluded from citizenship in Israel and foreigners to the covenants of the promise, without hope and without God in the world" (Ephesians 2:12).

Think about a love relationship between a husband and wife. During courtship, they cannot do enough for each other. Spending time together is a high priority, yet they have a mutual respect for their partner's schedule and physical, emotional, and spiritual needs. They hold each other in high regard. In some relationships, however, the desire to make sacrifices to please each other diminishes. Children are born, work hours increase, and community involvement often fills the remaining time for many busy people, so they spend even less time with their spouse. The result is a fragile relationship that lacks both depth and intimacy because they are preoccupied with other things.

Spiritual relationships work much the same way. People lose their appetite for God when their lives become full of other activities—work, volunteering, hobbies, TV, surfing the internet, and social media affairs. When we let activities prevent us from prioritizing time for fellowship with God, it affects our desire to please him. Not interacting with God in quiet time lessens our appetite for his presence until we do not desire to pursue him. Our relationship then becomes fragile, lacking depth and the intimacy God wants to have with us.

Does this describe you? Has your schedule become so busy that you think you don't have time to fellowship with God? There's a saying that if you're too busy for God, you're too busy. That is so true. While we're juggling all our tasks each day, God is saying, "I miss my time with you."

The apostle Paul wrote that all things are permissible, but not all things are profitable (1 Corinthians 10:23-24). That can include our schedules. Yes, many activities are permissible, but not all are profitable for our spiritual maturity. Read and meditate on this Scripture in a different translation now and again later as you are led by the Spirit: "All things are legitimate (permissible—and we are free to do anything we please), but not all things are helpful (expedient, profitable, and wholesome). All things are legitimate, but not all things are constructive [to character] and edifying [to spiritual life]" (1 Corinthians 10:23 AMPC).

Perhaps evaluating your relationship with God will help you identify why your appetite for him has diminished. When you're not pursuing intimacy with God, his Spirit will seem distant. This is not because he has left you, in fact he is very present, but because you have not been available, your hearts no longer beat as one. It is during times like these that everything you attempt becomes harder to accomplish. Inspiration fades and insightful perspective loses optimism, impairing one's vision and goals.

There will be times when projects and goals will completely fail. It is often those kinds of experiences that cause people to realize they are spiritually exhausted from trying to carry the weight of their world all alone. If you're feeling burdened, the weight you feel is caused by the distance you have placed between yourself and God. The Bible proclaims that the Lord has not forsaken them that seek him (Psalm 9:10). Commit to seek him, and you will learn to trust him with everything that concerns you.

SPIRITUAL SUBSTITUTES

The body requires consistent nutrition throughout the day. When we skip meals, hunger kicks in, and we may quickly eat any food that is easily available. Far too often, this includes junk food that provides little or no nutritional quality, even though they may bring temporary satisfaction. For some it is difficult to eat a balanced meal, and over time, poor diets and appetites can lead to severe health problems and even death in some instances.

In the same way, Christians who lose sight of their relationship with the Father experience a lack of spiritual nourishment, leading to destitution and spiritual death. This is manifested in a lack of power to activate faith, a sense of hopelessness, and doubt in God's love and ability to answer prayer. Neglecting one's covenant relationship breaks the bond with the source of all health and strength and is a form of disobedience that leads to seeking other sources as substitutes that become idols.

Choosing to experience the Bread of Life in a pause guarantees a healthy diet for spiritual well-being. Many substitutes can divert us from our responsibility to prioritize our covenant relationship, including good things such as ministry, career, school, friendships, and social and political trends. In recent years, we have seen how many individuals seek substitutions for immediate gratification and relationships through scrolling social media. What starts as a quick sixty seconds on Facebook, Instagram, or TikTok can turn into hours on these and other platforms, presenting a smorgasbord of unhealthy bites When ingested they curb emotions, but they're no not filling and create a desire for more. Regardless of the amount of time spent on these activities, they will never bring true satisfaction and spiritual growth.

Let me challenge you for one day to spend half the time you scroll social media prayerfully reading the Bible and being filled with the Spirit (Ephesians 3:19).

God knew that the enemy would use substitutions to interrupt moments of intimacy to attempt to break the covenant. This is why Jesus said, "It is written: 'Man shall not live on bread alone, but on every word that comes from the mouth of God'" (Matthew 4:4). In essence Christians must live a balanced life of consciousness of the presence of the Holy Spirit at all times. Social media, podcasts, YouTube, and other platforms can be used wisely, but they are not to replace our relationship building in his presence as the source of our life.

We have substituted many nouns—persons, places, and things—for God, made them into idols and given them the attention and affection that belongs to God. Distractions and temptations result when our hearts and minds are not focused wholeheartedly on his truth. Our senses are stimulated by the images and things we see, hear, and feel, even when we are not physically present, through devices like our phones, computers, and televisions. The odd thing is that a great amount of what we see is scripted and staged by others and is believable enough to influence us, our thoughts, and behavior unless we seek and apply wisdom and discernment.

Scrolling through social media to see and read a hot, spicy message or gossip item can distract and stimulate our senses for a moment but is useless in the midst of crises. Those times are when we must trust God and the truth of his Word stored in our hearts in the form of Scripture. Pressing pause in God's presence consistently provides content for our souls and spirits, giving hope that he is in control and at work on our behalf in every situation we face in real life.

Walking by faith can be difficult while living in a highly interactive, fast-paced world that so easily distracts us from the necessary time to experience his presence. The Scriptures give strength and guidance to navigate distractions, empowering us to walk by faith and not sight. The first commandment warned and prohibited making graven images as idols to worship. The children of Israel had no natural image of what God looked like, but this makes it clear that they were not supposed to make any items to bow down and worship. Perhaps God's intention was for all to learn and rely on his law, and not an image, by faith in him. However, the Israelites became distracted time after time and forgot God, suffering hardships because of disobedience and becoming servants to what they worshiped instead of God.

Do you feel broken, scattered, disturbed, or pulled all over the place? What are we distracted by that has made us break the covenant? What have we made ourselves slaves to? Is it career, pursuit of promotion, or gaining recognition for our platforms and other activities? What else comes to mind? Jeanne Karen Porter, a former superwoman who is a "recovering perfectionist," said, "We don't have to mask up and be more than we're supposed to be. We can draw from this inner strength that comes from that well of the Holy Spirit and from the cultural traditions that are given to us."[1] Inner strength is a result of making room in our day to maintain a healthy relationship with the Father.

QUIET TIME = DEEPER INTIMACY

A diminished appetite for God's presence leads to a diminished relationship with God and a mediocre life. On the other hand, a healthy appetite for the presence of God leads to victorious living. Quiet time with God equals a deeper relationship with him.

Jesus gave the key for success during his Sermon on the Mount, as recorded in Matthew 6:33. It says, "But seek ye first the kingdom of God, and his righteousness; and all these things shall be added unto you" (KJV). What things? All the material, physical, mental, emotional, and financial gains you are trying to achieve on your own. The schedule-fillers that crowd out time for relationship building with God have to be set aside to prioritize quiet time; then you can pursue the other things toward your goals and dreams.

Proverbs 3:5 tells us that we can learn to rely on God with our whole heart, and he will direct our path. Once we make a decision to love and obey him with a pure and sincere heart, we will see the power of his presence in every effort we make. The evidence may appear small at first, but keep pressing to regain fellowship with God. Eventually the desire to please God will become the top priority in your life each day.

To grow in intimacy with God, it is essential that we pray, read the Bible, and seek God daily for direction. Without doing those things, the believer will become weak and spiritually malnourished. The psalmist testifies in Psalm 34:4, "I sought the LORD, and he answered me; he delivered me from all my fears." Like the psalmist, you will have struggles in life that produce fear, but as the Word tells us, we can seek the Lord and he will hear us.

We all need God's love, but we often find other things or people filling the place in our heart that should belong to him. What are you substituting for his love? Some try to satisfy their need for God's love with sex, drugs, tobacco, alcohol, money, friends, or their job. Your life can be filled with seemingly good things, but if they keep you from devoting time to God, they are compromising your most important relationship.

SEE GOD AT WORK

First Corinthians 1:27 tells us that God can use the simple things to confound the wise, and that is indeed true. For example, when you pray because you lack the natural ability to accomplish a task and God gives you the grace to complete that task, it is amazing and increases your faith and trust in God. The Scripture in Psalm 34:8 enlivens you to "taste and see" the goodness of the Lord. You will begin to sense the presence of God more and more as you learn to trust him, love him, and believe his Word. Quiet time is all about building a relationship. It is just that simple.

It may seem like the items that have been served on your plate of life are distasteful—the deadlines, domestic issues, financial crunches, and health concerns. But pray over the situation ("meal") and ask God to encourage you to meditate on ("eat") the Word for strength to pursue his will. You have victory because the battle is not yours; it is the Lord's (2 Chronicles 20:15). When you trust God, in faith, the battle is already won. You are victorious! Jeremiah 29:11 says, "'For I know the plans I have for you,' declares the LORD, 'plans to prosper you and not to harm you, plans to give you hope and a future.'" Your future is victorious. Know that because of the Lord, you are a mighty person, full of hope and power as you satisfy your appetite in his Word.

Waking up to pray and read your Bible each morning may be challenging initially, but over time it will become easier because your passion for God's presence will increase. Commit to spend time each day praying, reading the Bible, and praising and worshiping God. Let these activities be the "main course" of your day. Don't become satisfied with all the other important life issues and forget the primary item that nourishes your spirit and soul.

Choose today to serve your spirit and soul the Word of God in the stillness of quiet each day, so you can continue developing a deeper relationship with Christ. This relationship will help you walk in confidence every day, as you affirm God's plans and love for you by memorizing and meditating on the Scriptures. Press pause with me and read about those who routinely found time for God and gained spiritual strength and insight (Abraham, Genesis 19:27; David, Psalm 5:3; even Mary the mother of Jesus, Acts 1:14 and Luke 1:46-55). Who would you like to pattern your life after?

PAUSE ON PURPOSE 7

ARE YOU HUNGRY?

But now we have lost our appetite; we never see
anything but this manna! – NUMBERS 11:6

In the race for promotion, productivity, and the world's idea of success, we can get caught in the trap of complaining about tasks that interrupt our personal work—in particular, time honoring our directives to seek God first. There were many times I wanted to convince myself that three hours on Sunday or two hours in church Bible study was enough. Especially in seasons of an active speaking schedule, medical vocation, family, and church membership responsibilities. There was no extra time for God. To be honest, this is when I found myself complaining about the meal God had prepared for me in Scripture.

I substituted listening to Christian YouTube podcasts and audiobooks for my time dedicated to God. It was not acceptable. It was a Cain offering to the Lord. My attention was divided, my spirit was not fully attuned to those messages, and there was minimal engagement with the Lord. Our relationship was rocky because my appetite no longer found pause in his presence to be tasteful.

Private time in pause might sound and at times feel challenging, even undesirable in the beginning, because the flesh doesn't want to submit to obedience to God. It is a sacrifice. As you commit and begin to see the benefits of clarity, focus, peace, long-suffering, and elimination of anxiety with productivity, the value will be revealed. In pause, you will find yourself adoring God with thanksgiving, praise, and spiritual maturity.

For many, it took a national pause during the Covid-19 pandemic to give our attention to God. We were forced into moments of pause. We prayed, rested, eliminated house items, and ate healthily—what happened when the sanction was lifted?

Evaluate your spiritual satisfaction. Have you lost your appetite for prayer and the Word? Are you prioritizing activities that suppress your appetite for God? Review your schedule today to determine when and where to begin quiet time. You can find in appendix D a prayer model to use to jumpstart your time with God in prayer.

Reflection: Irritability and other emotions of imbalance can be traced to the lack of consistency of personal spiritual care. Christians with a healthy appetite regularly spend time at Jesus' feet. There are times spiritual manna is not tasty, but it is beneficial for our spirit.

Prayer: Lord, my cup is empty. I come boldly to your throne for strength, to submit, trust, and embrace your grace of all sufficiency. I am hungry . . . Fill my cup till it overflows. Amen.

8

WELCOME TO THE TABLE

Here I am! I stand at the door and knock. If anyone hears my voice and
opens the door, I will come in and eat with that person, and they with me.

REVELATION 3:20

As A VISIONARY, it is easy for me to formulate a plan in my head
and put it on paper, and before I know it, implementation is in process.
Most of my sister-friends are this way. When we get together for a
peer mentoring meetup at a favorite coffee shop, where the sky is *not*
the limit for ideas, there are no boundaries to our imagination or time.
Until someone says, "I am exhausted," and someone else asks, "Is this
idea taking me in the direction God is calling?" The typical response
is that God would not have given these gifts and ideas if they had not
been part of our purpose. But do we have to attempt them all at once?

Sitting around the table with our laptops, planners, papers, and
phones out causes me to wonder how many of us really are considering
God's will in our plans for our lives, or even scheduling regular time,
designated appointments with him, among all the other scheduled
activities on our to-do lists.

One day, in the middle of loud chattering and clanking cups and
spoons, I calmly shared a suggestion: "Without judgment, guys, let's
do a scheduled inventory of our lives over the past two weeks to look

for direct quiet times of pause with God. Not a quick 'Lord, I thank you for a new day,' but quality time of fifteen to thirty minutes of prayer and Scripture reading?" There were stares and shifting in seats while looking at wristwatches or phones, and silence hovered over the table. Finally, one person said, "I am not a church leader or preacher like some of you." That was an interesting observation, given that all at the table were Christian women with active roles in the church. Are pastors the only ones responsible for studying the Bible and praying?

Since this was my suggestion, I was vulnerable with the group to share my discovery regarding the amount of time I had been scheduling myself, and I found seven out of fourteen days of time with God in prayer, Bible reading, and reflective journaling. My investigation showed that the first week was four days of scheduled time with God, and the second week was only three days of direct time with God. I am sure there were fleeting moments of communication during the other seven days, but not full attention in a posture of pause and solitude; I am sure that I prayed, called on his assistance, and even made biblical affirmation, but it still meant I missed my time with God. The same person who announced she was not a leader in the church then said, "Girl! Not you." Yes, me.

Even with the best intentions, if we are not alert to our spiritual needs, we can unconsciously be driven to the point of having limited or no time for God. We all have a desire to live life significantly, yet we need to set boundaries around our spiritual treasure of presence to stay balanced in all aspects of our lives. I shared that when there is an imbalance in priority, there comes a spiritual, mental, and physical homeostatic interruption in our focus, increased irritability, internal dis-ease, and a decrease in overall productivity. This started a massive conversation about time management for the total person, beginning with quiet time for the spiritual component and how it seems to be personal and a form of emotional intelligence.

The coffeehouse discussion changed from business and ministry projects to questions about how to create space for God, how to meet him at the table. The first step is to extend grace and patience to our-selves. As I tell myself and my patients, it is important not to beat ourselves up when we realize we have missed the mark in any area of our life. God is merciful and is waiting for us to return to him. He is ready whenever we are ready to accept the invitation and let him in as Father and partner to fulfill life purposes.

The second step is to make time in an overscheduled life, taking an honest look at your current schedules and eliminating appointments that are space holders—ones you know you should have never com-mitted to. Prayerfully consider a morning time and some random times once a day for a week, and see how unhampering and guilt-free it is to reset in pause with God. Pause and try this concept for two days, then follow the previous instructions for a week. Share how productive you became when you had regular time with God.

FINDING STILLNESS IN SOLITUDE

Before the Covid-19 pandemic, I thought I was disciplined with my prayer life. Although Covid-19 came with many traumatic stories, deaths, lost jobs, and cultural reconstructions, it was eye-opening for me in terms of my spiritual development. It allowed time to regain focus as to why I am a Christian. It is to imitate the life of Christ to build the kingdom of God, as we impact the lives of others with mercy and the compassion of Christ to provoke them to yield their lives to him. There is more to Christianity than the many benefits of being a follower of Christ, but the chief purpose is to represent the kingdom.

The pandemic forced a shutdown of almost the entire world in a mode of stillness. It taught me to seek more solitude and to lean into my relationship with God with a renewed passion for obeying God and practicing quietness of heart. There are many approaches to the practice of stillness; however, we can identify two primary types of stillness in solitude to begin exercising pause in our daily routine.

1. *Quiet time:* This is a brief daily act of pause—stillness in solitude—which should be practiced regularly, and reviewed and reflected on during the day.

2. *Personal retreats:* These are extended intervals of stillness in solitude that can be as short as a half-day or as long as several full days. This retreat can include fasting.

In either period of solitude, we are allowed to remove the mask. I like how Henri Nouwen describes his freedom in solitude: "I get rid of my scaffolding."[1] Many objects support the façade that we are self-sufficient, but in solitude, there are no phone calls, texts, emails, friends, or work commitments to fill our heads with vain words. When we remove ourselves from the hurriedness of daily tasks, we can be released from the infrastructure that supports our continuous running in the fast lane, feeding our ego, fostering our impostor syndrome, and keeping up with those around us.

Spiritual discipline is the core of a godly lifestyle for believers. It is not the fashions we spend time planning to buy, shopping for the best sale, and wearing to impress others for a few hours in a religious setting. Spiritual discipline is a foundation for living a full life of harmony with God, self, and man. Learning to practice quietness strengthened me during the tough times of my life. Because of the level of trust in God to rescue me by honoring his word, I learned how to manage my peace as I waited—and I am still waiting in some cases for God's hand to move concerning my prayer requests. Time with God is not just for a routine chat with the Father, but to become the transformed image of truth for a world that rejects a lifestyle of holy living. The discipline of pause is a space that infuses our moral compass with assurance and truths that guide our lives.

During my revelation of a greater need to practice separateness from the world, there were times of feeling guilt and even remorse for time missed with God, family, and friends because I was entwined in things I thought were necessary for serving God. They were not bad things, but good busyness that needed time restrictions. For example, during the Covid-19 pandemic, I did a rough estimation of how I spent my time and energy. The finding was that while working a full-time job, I was volunteering in ministry and community organizations that required nearly full-time hours. It was a startling discovery. Yes, I burned out with good busyness, and I had to learn to delegate and decline requests.

Around the coffee shop table that day, some of the women shared their burnout in current church work and admitted this was embedded theology, learned behavior. We saw granny, auntie, and momma do it, and thought we had to do it the same way. Juggling our families, careers, and exhausting servanthood assignments had become a trigger of homeostatic imbalance. The imbalance often led to mental, emotional, and physical power outages, and we needed to practice self-care to better manage our tasks.

JOINING MARY AT JESUS' FEET

We read in Luke 10:38-42 about Mary and Martha. Jesus visited the home of the sisters, and Martha was working as the hostess while Mary was sitting at Jesus' feet. One can surmise many reasons for their choices in the narrative. I would suggest that Martha was doing what was culturally expected of her, and that was serving in the capacity of hospitality. She perhaps lost track of time serving and cleaning with other things on her mind. Mary was sitting with Jesus, learning from him.

The text does not say, but I would like to diagnose the state of Martha as having symptoms of "dis-ease"—spiritual, emotional, and physical fatigue. It is characterized by irritability, malaise, and a poor perspective of others' behavior—the way Martha approached Jesus about Mary's unavailability to assist with preparation. Is it possible that she lost sight of her emotional awareness, spiritual hunger, and physical need for rest? Mary chose to refresh at the feet of Jesus. Could it have been that Martha was doing the most, like many of us when we are in overdrive?

Reading the narrative of Mary and Martha, it appears that Martha was not jealous of her sister, but sincere in wanting to please her guests as much as possible; however, she had a greater need within herself. One might suggest that Martha's insight was blurred when she criticized Mary for not helping, instead of making her own choice to take a break with Jesus before continuing to serve. Look at the passage with the mindset of a private investigator:

> "Martha, Martha," the Lord answered, "you are worried and upset about many things, but few things are needed—or indeed only one. Mary has chosen what is better, and it will not be taken away from her." (Luke 10:41-42)

Emphatically, Jesus' tone teaches that *Mary chose the better thing, and I am not going to interrupt her to assist you.* Implicitly, the invitation to pause was extended to Martha: to stop working on what she was doing and come join Mary. Can you sense his love and release of guilt inviting Martha to choose the better way? I think Jesus was encouraging balanced behavior, suggesting there is a time and season for serving and a time for refreshing. What is the one thing needed to reset balance in your relationship with God? What is the best thing that you can do?

Becoming spiritually disciplined is a choice. If you, like me, have chosen to serve in too many organizations at your church, work, or ministry, forgive yourself now and be free to say no. If you are upset with the ministry leadership team for not relieving you of excessive duties or not recruiting someone else to help, forgive and release them.

We live in a world that is all about choices. So often, women don't notice how full their plate of responsibility is until stress ensues. Women usually disregard warning signs in their bodies, especially their emotions and spiritual outcries for pause. This is a frequent observation in the healthcare setting. We often associate anxiety with impending feelings of being overwhelmed before going to the emergency room or our primary care doctor. The feeling of dis-ease (stress) is an internal alarm triggered by our bodies to make us aware that something is out of whack. When this imbalance remains uncorrected, it can lead to more anxiety, high blood pressure, headaches, chest pain, depression, dry skin or a rash, the manifestation of cancer, heart disease, or other chronic illnesses.

The women at the table in the coffee shop that day decided to select accountability partners and agreed not to add anything else to their schedule without consulting with one another. The decision was also made to prioritize current appointments and remove one item off the schedule daily for two weeks to provide time for God and self.

Then the women decided to meet in two weeks instead of the next quarter to see how this plan worked. They found one of the main areas of improvement was the relationship with family or spouse and better consistency in private time with God. The second area was that muting morning calls during time with God and family time prevented responses and verbal commitments that generally added to their schedule. One participant voiced she now had time to refresh her mind with notes from journaling and reflecting on the morning Scriptures throughout the day.

RELYING ON BIBLICAL PRINCIPLES

Coming to the table means meeting with the Father regularly to learn biblical standards, which has a greater impact than relying on positive affirmations. Social media is filled with positive affirmations that have shallow returns. Hope is built on faith that embraces the promise of truth. It is up to each person whether they will learn Scripture or hold total dependence on positive affirmations that offer temporary hope.

The use of biblical principles is necessary for effective Christian living. This is seen in Jesus' responses after his forty-day fast and being tempted by Satan in the wilderness (Matthew 4:1-11), and in dealing with the religious and political leaders challenging and trying to find fault in him (John 5). We may not be fasting in the wilderness, but many temptations distract us from putting God first. There are work, school, church, and community obligations that can misguide our priorities if we are not aware of the needs of our spiritual health.

Consumers select restaurants according to their cravings for the desired type of food, atmosphere, and in some cases the health benefits. Spiritual mealtimes and appetite choices appear to be based on religious belief systems. In both instances, choices are most often based on cultural trends.

> Religious beliefs are indicators of what people believe about God, Jesus, the Bible, angels, demons, miracles, Salvation, Heaven, Hell, life after death, and our relationship with God. These indicators provide insight into our Biblical belief system.
>
> Our understanding of Scripture, or lack thereof, forms our opinions on what is right and wrong and what is true and false. Without question, Biblical illiteracy is taking its toll on America. Only 51 percent of our pastors and 6 percent of Americans continue to hold a Biblical worldview.[2]

How a person perceives the need for God often determines the priority of honoring the invitation to schedule a time to dine with him. God is always available for you to start a new relationship with him or restore a fractured relationship. A loving Father is waiting for his children. As it says in Jeremiah: "Therefore thus says the LORD, 'If you return, then I will bring you back; you shall stand before Me'" (Jeremiah 15:19 NKJV).

Bible reading has always been a place of peace and hope for me, even as a child, and especially when I was given Sunday school lesson cards. With the images characterizing the lesson in my small hands, it was as if I were a part of the story, and the words were so alive that my faith grew as a child. I collected them and savored what I felt was the voice of God in my little hands, believing every word.

It is never too late to spend quiet time in God's presence. There is no need to condemn yourself for losing your appetite for God. Pause is a source of reset into spiritual homeostasis, and this chapter offers steps and practical strategies to streamline your schedule to make room for God. Whether new to the process or restarting your relationship with God, you will become more productive after spending time with God.

PAUSE TO PURSUE MORE OF GOD

After leaving the lady bosses' time of project peer mentoring that day in the coffee shop, I was more aware of my disconnectedness from God. I went home and put on my walking clothes but was still worried about many things. While on my backyard deck, I watched a red cardinal come and sit on the banister, so close I could see its eyes as it flew away. It was like it had a message, but we could not communicate. Then I took a long walk near the lake on the walking trail and was welcomed by a swarm of cardinals. What did this mean? Sitting on a bench, I used my phone to search up the meaning of seeing a red bird. Even though I knew this trail from walking it frequently, I had never had this type of "bird" experience.

There are many variations of the spiritual meaning of seeing a red bird based on cultural or religious traditions. The primary meanings that resonated with me were a spiritual awakening, transformation, a message of hope, and restoration "for emotional and spiritual healing, leading to growth within the individual and helping them in times of trouble with a clear mindset."[3]

That day, I needed a touch from God. I desired a spiritual awakening like the day I experienced my new birth in Christ. Yes, I had been praying, reading my Bible, and journaling all the usual things, but something was missing. The barrenness of my spirit was directly related to my lack of full attention to God. I was doing all the right things to be successful in society, but my productivity in the kingdom of God was near a halt, and there was no peace.

FRESH START

Growing up in New England, I became accustomed to watching boats and barges as they were guided into port to unload or refuel in preparation for another trip. If they did not stop for rest, they would run out of fuel, the crew would be exhausted, and at worst, the vessel would crash. Thus, the captain and crew had to follow the guidelines to ensure the vessel and crew had the necessary gear for the next voyage.

God has made provision for a new beginning, a fresh start for you who are spiritually exhausted, dry, sinful, weary, burned out, distant from God, and unable to discern his presence. I have experienced the same feelings on many occasions due to being in motion with what seemed like no time to pause with him.

The Bible has many examples of individuals who needed a fresh start. There is David, who committed adultery and murder. In disobedience and fear of doing an assignment, Jonah ran from God, but he was given a chance of a fresh start. It was a new beginning for Peter after denying Christ not once but three times. How many times have we disregarded engaging God because we were too busy?

God is waiting to welcome us back as he prepares the table in the presence of our enemies (Psalm 23:5). Saul, whose name was changed to Paul, was forgiven and given a new ministry after persecuting the church.

Where are you? How would you categorize your time with God? If you have no time or plenty of time, he is still faithful to forgive us and give us a fresh start, like the water vessels and biblical characters are given a fresh start (1 John 1:9). Pray and ask God to forgive you for missing time with him and neglecting your relationship. This is just between you and the Father.

We take the opportunity every New Year to make resolutions to begin a fresh start in different areas. Think about what we do in preparation for the New Year regarding the proposed or desired changes we want to make in our lives. Some people do vision board parties, house reorganization, plan new diets, or hire personal trainers. There is no question we want a fresh start, but I have come to the realization that attempting too many changes at once creates further fragmentation in our day-to-day routines.

Our jam-packed schedules include additional truckloads of burdens related to family, career, ministry, and community, and our work as natural nurturers can get weighed down in the sea of despair when we take on much more than we can bear. God sees and is merciful, but we have to be wise in doing the work. Press pause, look at your schedule, eliminate nonessential meetings, and block out time for the Lord.

U-TURN PERMITTED

Have you ever been driving in an unfamiliar place and suddenly realized that you are going in the wrong direction, but at the next opportunity to turn around, there was a sign that read "U-turn not permitted"? Fortunately, on this Christian journey, we can always make the necessary changes—even U-turns—to grow in holiness. If you have not been able to develop a deeper relationship with God and experience the benefits of being an heir of Christ, it is not too late to make a U-turn.

The demands and expectations of life can be overwhelming at times, with seemingly incessant commitments to family, work, school, church, and civic organizations. It can seem impossible to lessen the load. But as a Christian, you can always go to God and ask for help. You can start over. I am not saying this will not involve adjustments, but know that you can make changes that will benefit your relationship with God.

You may be an individual who accepts many tasks but never seems to start or to complete them. For example, you may purchase a new book and stop reading it, begin a personal Bible study and never get past day one, or join a community Bible study group and never attend. Maybe you have begun the Christian walk but seem to have made little progress. Or perhaps you have become faint-hearted and have given up on serving the Lord.

Does it seem that you are always starting over in your Christian walk, but never get over the obstacles to move into maturity? If you have not understood Bible teachings in Sunday school, Saturday school, Bible study, or worship service, you must grasp the fact that the devil is a dirty fighter. He does not play fair; he deliberately attacks your weaknesses. He does not want you to understand and learn Scripture. He wants you weaponless. This is why the Word teaches us in Ephesians 4:27 not to give place to the devil.

If you're scratching your head and wondering, "What is this woman talking about?" let me make it plain. You wake up every morning with an agenda that is either disregarded or never attempted because of an unrealistic schedule, lack of interest, lack of preparation, fear, doubt, or incomplete direction from God. Midway through your day you realize that your shoulders are heavy, the midline of your neck is tight, and your eyes are blurred. You think out loud, "There has to be a better way."

Yes, there is a path you can take that will lead you to greener pastures. You follow it by submitting to the will of the Father. Your obedience to becoming a student of the Word and a worshiper in spirit and truth leads to a better way to face daily challenges.

Proverbs 14:12 reads, "There is a way that seems right to a man, but its end is the way to death." The Shepherd's hands must direct your every move. Then you can quote Psalm 23 with conviction. He really will be your Shepherd. You won't have unmet needs. You won't fear, because your relationship with God will give you assurance that he is always present. Decisions and planning will become easier as you allow God to direct you in prayer and his Word.

Do you have a plan but don't know what to do with it? First of all, submit yourself and your plan to the Lord. Then he will direct your path. Many people are exhausting themselves trying to do things their own way. If that describes you, take the advice of Proverbs 3:5-6 and "trust in the LORD with all your heart, and lean not on your own understanding, in all your ways submit to him and he will make your path straight." There is no need to struggle when you are a child of God.

Learn to start your daily journey with the Lord and watch the Lord's favor prosper you in all that you attempt to do. If you have made a mess of things, repent and ask God to help you turn from those blunders. Refocus your energy in the direction that guarantees victory. Be confident of this, "he who began a good work in you will carry it on to completion until the day of Christ Jesus" (Philippians 1:6).

In Philippians 3:12, Paul states: "Not that I have now attained [this ideal], or have already been made perfect, but I press on to lay hold of (grasp) and make my own, that for which Christ Jesus (the Messiah) has laid hold of me and made me His own" (AMPC). Regardless of the road you've traveled in life, you can proceed in victory. You may be dealing with sin, shame, sickness, poverty, domestic disputes, emotional upheaval, procrastination, or a total deferment of your dreams, but you still can be free. You can maintain peace until God manifests your desire. Yes, we learn the skill of patience too as favor is demonstrated.

Take some time out during the upcoming week to read Ephesians 4:17-32. It teaches some interesting truths that, if applied, will enable you to walk in renewed strength. You do not have to remain entangled in your old habits. God is waiting for you to change direction to obtain power to accomplish the task of living holy.

A U-turn is permitted, it's not too late. You can make your life better by submitting to Jesus Christ. Repent and turn away from anything that does not please the Father. I am not saying that you have to be perfect, but you will have to learn to keep working toward your purpose. It is his will that you be victorious in every aspect of your life.

Commit today to no longer allow your past to control your thought patterns or behavior. Remember, you are a new creature now that you have repented and accepted God's forgiveness. Old things have passed away (2 Corinthians 5:17). Make a U-turn today and press toward the mark of better days (Philippians 3:14). When you start pursuing a deeper relationship is up to you, but a better life and the fulfillment of your purpose begin with quiet time with God each day.

My search to know him and teach others how to experience meaningful baby action steps launched me on a quest to the personal practice of pausing in various ways for spiritual maturity. This practice resets spiritual homeostasis in the life of anyone who seek spirituality. It requires planning and committed execution for active interaction between the Bible and God. It will not happen all at once, but if you make time for him he will be waiting for you.

▋▋ PAUSE ON PURPOSE 8

DAY BY DAY

Because of the LORD's great love we are not consumed,
for his compassions never fail.
They are new every morning;
great is your faithfulness. – **LAMENTATIONS 3:22-23**

What is your routine in the mornings?

Scripture reading, journaling, and biblical affirmation have been the source of managing my attitude for my day. This habit of intimacy with God has helped boost a rhythm of consistent balance in my life. The act of practicing quiet time with God has enhanced my memory and overall physical and mental health.

Morning activities have a direct impact on how we approach the remainder of the day. Think about it: If there is an emergency, accident, or food spill, anything that disrupts the morning can create an adverse emotion and thought pattern throughout the day. This can bleed into how we think, act, and interact with others for the remainder of the day. Having time for stillness in the early morning before our day begins provides grounding for a perspective of hopefulness and God's assurance. He is present.

Spiritual saturation in the morning assures that we have a foundation of truth to access positive talk if the day becomes filled with chaos. Otherwise, chaos can provoke negative self-talk, poor eating, and irrational behavior.

What are some morning practices you can incorporate to prepare you for a day reflecting on God's assurance and truth?

Reflection: Spend some time today praying for God's guidance for your life as you commit to finding more time in prayer, Bible study, and worship. Write what God speaks to your heart in your quiet time journal.

Prayer: Father, I know you are near and desire my embrace. Help me organize myself to begin this commitment to build a relationship with you. Lord, I desire to mature spiritually . . . speak to my heart.

9

THE FAVOR OF GOD

For those who find me find life and receive favor from the LORD.

PROVERBS 8:35

SOCIETY'S FRENZY IN THE FAST LANE has trained us to approach God as if he is an ATM, a genie in a bottle who provides our wishes on command or manifests prayers immediately on demand. Neither approach bears a close relationship with God, and neither demonstrates intimacy, respect, or a sense of gratitude toward him. God is alive and should not be treated as an inanimate object that provides desires. How we honor our relationship with God determines how we interact with his people and gain access to blessings.

God's favor is about God's goodness in bestowing gifts of blessings as promised. The opportunity to receive gifts from God is accessible to all humankind. Like any covenant agreement, however, our salvation agreement has terms and conditions. God is not a taskmaster and has given us the free will to choose to be in a relationship with him. Obedience leads to his will being accomplished on the earth through us with a life of peace and fulfillment according to his plan. It makes favor, grace, and mercy follow us all the days of our lives. We are all endowed with a measure of faith (Romans 12:3) and born with irrevocable gifts (Romans 11:29).

FAVOR, GRACE, AND MERCY: ARE THEY THE SAME?

Favor and *grace* are often used interchangeably, but there is a difference. Grace is free, not earned. Favor, on the other hand, can be gained or deserved. Psalm 5:12 says, "Surely, LORD, you bless the righteous; you surround them with your favor as with a shield."

Favor is merited or unmerited. It is not an act of favoritism, as humans display, but a divine act of God using people to bless. Grace is a gift that we don't earn or deserve—unmerited. It's like a job opportunity we weren't fully qualified for or being allowed to purchase a new home when our credit score wasn't the best. We receive these blessings not because of our merit but because of God's grace.

Mercy is when one doesn't receive the penalty deserved. In the case of God's redemptive love, he sent his Son so that we might be forgiven from paying the price for our sins. Similarly, a natural judge may choose to drop bail or drop the case when a sentence for punishment should have been served.

We see individuals who love and serve God who are suffering, while some who do not profess love for God appear to be blessed with a comfortable lifestyle without struggles. Does this mean God loves one more than the other? What does this have to do with the purpose of pressing pause? The purpose and result of pause is threefold: (1) it ensures that we adopt the character of God as his children to let our light shine so that men see our good works and glorify him (Matthew 5:16); (2) it inspires others to accept Jesus as Savior; and (3) it draws others to hope in God.

Time with God is not about what we can get from him, but a transformative exchange occurs in us as we take on the expressed image of God and exhibit his characteristics in our daily lives. Mutual trust is built for confidence in following God's leading and his will in all areas of our lives. Psalm 90:17 says, "May the favor of the Lord our God rest on us; establish the work of our hands for us—yes, establish the work of our hands."

The benefit of pause reestablishes the original intention of intimacy with God in his plan for humankind to fellowship with him, and enjoy all creation together. As we learn the heart and character of God, we understand our spiritual birthrights as his children. The value of covenant and the exchange of expectations and responsibilities are agreed on. Trust develops in private time with God, and we learn how to experience him as an individual. Experiencing spirituality can be easier in a crowd at a worship service, but God also wants to spend individual time with us. It is a space where we turn and secure our gaze toward him with full affection.

THE BLESSINGS OF GOD

You may have heard people say, "Favor ain't fair." As popular as that saying is, it is not true. People often make that statement when one person appears more blessed than another. But favor is available to all believers who apply Scripture in faith as they live in obedience to the conditions of the promise.

This is why becoming familiar with the Scriptures in Bible study, prayer, and meditation is foundational to Christian living. Consistently reading God's Word helps us memorize Scriptures so we will be able to confess the appropriate verses based on what we are requesting in prayer or believing to be manifested. Confessing Scripture assists in affirming hope while we wait for the answer to our prayer. As we do this, we will begin to see the blessings of the Lord in our life and that of others. These blessings are not only material: good health, spiritual growth, and a balanced life are also blessings from the Lord. To maintain victory, we must practice godly living as revealed in the Bible, and we do this by spending time in God's Word.

The Bible encourages us to study the Word to show ourselves approved unto God as workmen that do not need to be ashamed (2 Timothy 2:15). And 2 Timothy 3:16 tells us that "all Scripture is God-breathed and is useful for teaching, rebuking, correcting and training in righteousness." Quiet time assists us in becoming practicing students of the Bible, which contains all criteria for spiritual growth and development.

As Christ matured physically and spiritually, it was evident that the favor of God was on his life. Luke 2:52 says, "And Jesus grew in wisdom and stature, and in favor with God and man." If Jesus had to mature and increase in wisdom, stature, and favor with God and man, how much more are we to be responsible for nurturing our spirit, soul, and body for the glory of God?

The results of quiet time are demonstrated in the manifestation of the fruit of the Spirit, wisdom, prosperity, and health, among other things. Engaging in private worship deepens our love relationship with God. The blessings of God that many call *favor* will be evident in those who have a growing relationship with him; therefore, favor *is* fair, if you are obedient to the principles of godly living. The Bible says in Deuteronomy 29:9, "You must carefully obey everything in this agreement so you will succeed in everything you do" (NCV). This is God's favor.

God appeared to Solomon and set forth criteria for him to obtain favor, and all Christians must meet them:

> If My people, who are called by My name, shall humble them-
> selves, pray, seek, crave, and require of necessity My face and turn
> from their wicked ways, then will I hear from heaven, forgive
> their sin, and heal their land. (2 Chronicles 7:14 AMPC)

Favor and God's blessings are often a result of obedience, while grace is God's unmerited favor. When you repent and turn from your sinful ways and seek the Lord, you can have confidence that God will hear you and heal your land (bless your life). Your healing need could be physical, emotional, or spiritual, but regardless of how it manifests, you can count on God to be faithful to his Word.

Active participation in quiet time promotes health to the spirit, soul, and body. This is accomplished because our mind begins to agree with truth, and the Holy Spirit ignites a flame of passion for life, stimu- lating a hunger and thirst to pursue godliness. Commitment to daily Bible study provokes us to seek healthy lifestyles to strengthen the body in order to preserve life and effectively serve God in the local community and the world.

If you are one of many who profess Christ as Lord of your life but have not utilized the power of quiet time, then, yes, you may feel that "favor ain't fair." Some live in sickness and poverty and experience multiple forms of trials because they have not submitted completely to God nor sought understanding of God's Word. To develop a deeper relationship with God, you must totally surrender to him and not give him only lip service for personal gain.

BE AWARE OF YOUR MOTIVES

Let me caution about becoming selfish and self-seeking, which leads to pride. The blessings can come so fast that pride can easily begin to manifest. It is a thin line between humility and false humility, just acting humble. Living a prayerful life will help us honor God by giving him all the glory for the blessings in our lives. During times of reflection, we evaluate our reasons for developing an intimate relationship with God. Is it to glorify him?

If you find that your motives are not pure, repent and believe that God has forgiven you. The Bible says, "If we confess our sins, He is faithful and just to forgive us our sins and to cleanse us from all unrighteousness" (1 John 1:9 NKJV). Remember, it's never too late to develop an incredible relationship with him!

Recalling the Scriptures during times of prayer, by affirming and confessing God's promises to his children, will enliven your prayer time. That is why I have included a list of Bible passages in the appendixes that will help you proclaim God's Word during your quiet time. Let these serve as a starting point that will only grow as you deepen your knowledge of Scripture.

HIS PRESENCE IS AVAILABLE

Pausing from your busy schedule in quiet time with the Lord helps you to become familiar with the Scriptures, which enable you to accept your God-given rights as a Christian. First Kings 2:3 says, "And keep the charge of the LORD thy God, to walk in his ways, to keep his statutes and his commandments, and his judgments, and his testimonies, as it is written in the law of Moses, that thou mayest prosper in all that thou doest" (KJV). Now that is favor!

Many of us face daily challenges not recognizing that God's presence is accessible. We have to learn how to spend time with him. Yes, even in the midst of what appears to be an unfavorable circumstance, we must learn to settle down and experience his presence, which will guide us. There have been times when I could not see my way out of a circumstance, and God would send a sign that comforted me. Psalm 86:17 is a verse we can confess in prayer during challenging times: "Show me a sign of your favor" (ESV).

Do you know people who attend church and experience worship, but fail to realize that they have been in the presence of God? In Luke 24:13-35, Jesus' disciples were on their way from Jerusalem to the village of Emmaus. They were walking with Jesus, but they were so preoccupied with his crucifixion and finding his tomb empty that they failed to realize who was walking with them. It is conceivable that perhaps they were so overwhelmed with their current affairs that they neglected the presence of the One they could have been consulting, worshiping, and praising. His presence was right there with them and was not acknowledged. They did not perceive that Jesus was walking with them. Are you so preoccupied with the affairs of life that you cannot perceive God's presence?

Many of us are in that place of wanting a successful life. We want the promotion, good health, wealth, and spiritual maturity. Unfortunately, because we fail to acknowledge God's presence or our lack of desire to spend time with him, we tend to live in mediocrity. We are afforded the opportunity to worship God freely in the United States, but many people take this blessing lightly.

If you have been struggling with developing intimacy with God, remember that regular time in prayer, Bible reading, and reflection in private and in public religious settings increases a passion for God. Pressing pause is like a personal retreat with God to rejuvenate faith and allow the Scriptures to manifest in daily life. For others, it will be the beginning of a fresh love relationship. As you allow yourself to be refreshed in God's presence, you will find what your daily schedule has been missing without daily quiet time with him. The exploration of the Bible will continue to unfold, showing you how much he loves you in every situation of your life. As his daughter, you will learn that when you have a foggy brain and are unclear, God will enable you with grace to obtain focus.

There were times during my earlier fifties when the oncologists induced chemical menopause, and my thoughts and health seemed uncertain. For nearly twenty-four months I had to live on the invisible strength of God's grace. In private, weakly singing of his love and power, I had to daily remind myself that God's grace was sufficient. I felt saturated in his presence, resting in knowing he would take care of me (2 Corinthians 12:9). There were times of deep loneliness when I was unable to say a word verbally, but I still found strength to write petitions to the Lord in my journal. As I checked off answered prayers in my journal, it became empowering and built my faith as I saw God restore me.

Throughout those moments of pause, God used the process of journaling to slow my mind down, release fear and doubt, and trust that he was at work behind the scenes for me and my family. In this phase of life I felt supernaturally pregnant, as if I were birthing something special, but I had no idea what was to be born. How many times have you had a vision that was so huge, no one else could imagine it materializing for you, yet nevertheless encouraging you to see it come to pass?

This is a good time to begin journaling, if you haven't been already, to process God's favor in your life. Since you have been praying and answering short questions after each of the previous chapters, this is a good time to slow down your thoughts and visibly recount favor on your life with God and man. Your pause on purpose today can assist you in identifying how God is at work in your life as a helper, friend, provider, comforter, and healer, and being present as Father—that's favor. Proverbs 8:35 says, "For those who find me find life and receive favor from the LORD."

Although I was suffering, the more I sought the Lord, the more he revealed himself to me, his assurance of a good outcome, and his love for me. The practice of pause is valuable to Christians to live peaceable and successful lives. In God's presence you learn that the accumulation of wealth is not the mark of favor but the sweet aroma of his presence that follows you all the days of your life. If you are searching in the "fast lane" for the fountain of life and the secrets to favor and success, lean into God's Word and you will find it.

I once saw in a museum a mural that depicted the piers along the waters of St. Petersburg, Florida, as the fountain of youth. God offers more than youth, but the secrets to favor that will sustain us through life, generations to come, and eternity. The passage of Proverbs 8:35 in the Passion translation says, "For the fountain of life pours into you every time that you find me, and this is the secret of growing in the delight and the favor of the Lord." There is no need to hurry in your pursuit of God.

A. W. Tozer noted that "God never hurries. There are no deadlines against which He must work. Only to know this is to quiet our spirits and relax our nerves."[1] Press pause in his presence and allow the Spirit to pour life into you. Experience a feeling of better strategies and creativity and live in love. Learn how to truly work smarter as you grow in the delight and the favor of the Father. In appendix A you will find a quick assessment to help you determine where you spend too much or too little time, in order to better prioritize your daily meeting time and schedule pause on purpose with God. You will use these results also for your self-care plan in chapter eleven.

PAUSE ON PURPOSE 9

SETTING PRIORITIES

Let the morning bring me word of your unfailing love,
for I have put my trust in you.

Show me the way I should go,

for to you I entrust my life. – PSALM 143:8

The cost of travel, registration, and a hotel for professional development can be expensive in any profession. Sitting in the hospital cafeteria, my colleagues and I were talking about what it takes as well as the price we continue to pay to maintain our credentials. Christian spiritual development has a price paid for in full by the Son of God who died to redeem us and provide abundant life on earth and eternity in heaven.

The price we owe is to seek him first. Prioritizing time with the Father is the source of maintaining our relationship with the Lord. Some only make use of God for what they can get for selfish gain. Time with God is not an act of looking into a crystal ball to know the future, but a divine systematic strategy to prepare us for the day with strength, sharpening our thought process and enlivening our spirit.

With your Bible, journal, and planner in hand, direct guidance for your day becomes clear as the Spirit of God helps you select your best-suited time. "The LORD is with [you]; he is [your] helper. [You can] look in triumph on [your] enemies" (Psalm 118:7). Before attempting your next task, consider trying quiet time for an excellent outcome. Pause is a preparatory resource to sharpen your skills. There is a saying from an anonymous lumberjack: "If his life depended upon his ability to cut down a tree in five minutes, he would spend three minutes sharpening his axe."

Reflection: Prioritizing time in God's presence sharpens wisdom, trust, and love, for others and self. Then we can increase productivity at home, at work, and in community service and have time to enjoy abundant living.

Prayer: Lord, turn my affections toward you. Take control of my life. When I awake in the morning, let my heart seek your face first as I rest in peace, knowing that you care for me as you do the birds in the air.

10

SPIRITUAL DIRECTION AND DIVINE PROTECTION

The angel of the LORD encamps around those
who fear him, and he delivers them.

PSALM 34:7

PAUSE IN THE QUIET TIME builds a spiritual fort of protection around us and our families and strengthens us for battle. Intimacy with the Father prepares us for spiritual warfare in daily life. It is a protective device that keeps us aware of the power of prayer for our family, friends, health, work, and life processes. The increased movement in our lives can diminish our spiritual and natural awareness of the adversary's tactics, affording the enemy to creep in and lay traps—little foxholes to gain footholds.

During times of pause, the revelation of God's Word becomes alive and more relevant with knowledge of how and when to apply particular Scriptures, prayer, and faith to guide us through turbulent spaces. Trusting and following the leading of the Holy Spirit will give hope and assurance during times of crisis or spiritual warfare. Jesus told us trials will come, so there is no need to be caught off guard. He has a solution to overcome every situation we face. As we keep our end of the covenant agreement, we learn that trials are times to expect God to present himself strong and keep his promises as we stand fully armed in battle. Quiet times are the entrance into praise and worship, which invite the Spirit of God to rest on us, refreshing and filling our hearts with hope.

Spiritual direction and divine protection are a part of the heritage of the family of God. Access to the Father for guidance in decision-making is available in prayer, reading, and reflection, when we are still long enough in the presence of the Holy Spirit. The Holy Spirit might inspire us directly; perhaps someone might call us or see us in the store, and a conversation on the issue at hand is sparked that leads to a solution in which the person had no idea of the dilemma.

Push the pause button now. What's troubling your heart? In his presence, there is wisdom, joy, and comfort in the guidance of his presence.

PAUSE IN MOTION

Author and theologian Howard Thurman observed,

> It is good to make an end of movement, to come to a point of rest, a place of pause. There is some strange magic in activity, in keeping at it, in continuing to be involved in many things that excite the mind and keep the hours swiftly passing. But it is a deadly magic; one is not wise to trust it with too much confidence.
>
> The moment of pause, the point of rest, has its own magic.[1]

To keep the human body functioning effectively in crisis, there is a "flight or fight" response for survival physiologically, which occurs in a stressful or urgent situation and is a type of pause to reset and maintain homeostasis for normal bodily functions.

Christians who practice one of many forms of contemplative quiet time soon learn the power of pause to determine whether to activate fight in prayer and Scriptures or take flight and request the church elders or others for prayer in circumstances too heavy to bear. Grounding our relationship with our Father before any battle is an opportunity to readily recognize the nearness of God in peace before being at the point of duress.

In moments of pause, we increase our spiritual awareness and emotional intelligence. Christian growth and development, when done correctly, fosters a healthy, spiritually mature individual. These persons model a life of spiritual intelligence, which is the awareness of the closeness of God's presence and the ability to effectively discern the works of Satan. Spiritually healthy individuals have keen insight into God's protective power, overshadowing and covering them during adversity. They don't abandon their faith, nor fear easily succumbing to the enemy's antics. They trust the relationship with the Lord, which is developed in private time together. Think about the three Hebrew boys in Daniel 3; they came out untouched, not even smelling of smoke—hidden, protected in the presence of the fourth man in the fire (Daniel 3:19-25). They trusted God.

We are promised that "whoever dwells in the shelter of the Most High will rest in the shadow of the Almighty" (Psalm 91:1). There are many examples of God's divine sovereignty that become visible the more we bond with him. One December, my family and I traveled to Connecticut by car—my husband driving, my sister in the front seat, our son and a new baby girl with me in the back. On the turnpike, changing baby girl's diaper, I peered between the seats and saw my husband was asleep. I screamed his name, startling him, and he overcorrected on a sheet of ice. The car began spinning like a bottle on a table. We saw the cargo carrier atop our Subaru wagon become unstrapped and fly near the guardrail. We both screamed, "Jesus!"

It was as if the hand of God was placed on the top of the car when it came to a complete stop in the middle of the highway. It was odd that no cars were coming; we were the only car on that side of the interstate. My husband tried to start up the car, but it would not after several attempts. I looked back and could see the morning rush coming in the distance. Suddenly an army truck filled with soldiers pulled up and parked beside our car. Soldiers jumped out of the truck, pushed our car over to the right of the interstate toward the guardrail, and placed our carrier on the right-hand front bumper.

We looked at each other when we heard the rush of cars speeding past us in all lanes. We were flabbergasted, trying to figure out how, when, and where all those soldiers came from, and where they did they go? We did not see the trucks drive off and leave. Just a rush of cars in what was a four lane interstate. Sitting there checking the children, our daughter had only a superficial skull laceration. I was grateful the pillow was on the floorboard behind the driver's seat where she fell. Shortly after, we heard sirens and the EMTs came to make general assessments and transport us to the emergency room to be evaluated. This was an act of divine intervention for the protection of my family.

There are many times in my life and possibly yours when we can remember that God provided us with spiritual direction and protection. In moments of stillness, we can best learn and reflect on God's goodness. Those are the times when we are grateful and without question acknowledge that there is an invisible war going on that cannot be fought with natural hands alone.

SPIRITUAL WARFARE IS REAL

Motion picture cinematography features evil winning and immorality being tolerated. This has added a subtle message to doubt or disregard the existence of God and Satan. The silent messages can disarm the alertness and active use of spiritual weapons among Christians. One of the primary weapons is growth in the Word. When we fail to spend regular time in the Word, we cannot remember how to accurately combat the attacks of darkness that aim to steal, kill, and destroy.

If you have not experienced temptation, there will come a time when the evil one will tempt you. It might be as harmless as distracting you with overcommittment, a prideful disposition, or an overzealous desire for fame and fortune. These are tricks of war to disarm you to disregard your spiritual sonship and skew your view of your covenant with the Father. Remain strong and focused in faith through consistent engagement, reviewing God's battle plan for victorious living.

Never allow yourself to ignore your spiritual relationships with God; it is a part of the blueprint for divine direction and protection. The subtle diversions when we pursue our dreams can distract us, making it easy to compromise. The reality is spiritual warfare is ongoing, and as Christians it's important to press pause as a significant source of our effectiveness in dismantling the works of the devil.

In the marketplace, we are intentional about networking. It is a form of relationship building for expansion, platform growth, and new connections. We schedule meetups before and after work, even after a long day at the office. Why? We know networking is a significant part of growth and development. One can look at networking as a type of covenant formation. Think about it: Some of the best partnerships and deals are made on the golf course or at a professional development workshop. To solidify the partnership, trust, and confidence, time together fuels the relationship's success. The covenant we have with God is all-inclusive. It contains more than we can ask, think, or imagine, only if we seek him wholeheartedly.

The more we communicate with God in a posture of pause, we will sense the prompting of the Holy Spirit and move confidently in the good times and tough times, watching God keep his promises. We will learn that God loves us and that he hears our cry. Whether we are screaming with joy or crying tears from the hurt and pain of life, our time with him will undergird us in peace to take action when the Holy Spirit gives us the green light to go forward with a task at hand. Our cry doesn't have to be out of fear, disappointment, and despair, but it can be a cry out to him in reverence and thanksgiving.

We can spend hours mulling over thoughts that reveal indecisiveness because of a fragmented heart. When we seek God wholeheartedly, we will find him and embrace him as a friend and Lord, accepting our rightful positions as Christians. Although there are times I have felt overwhelmed, tearful, and afraid, the posture of stillness has sustained me as I learned to rest in truths to combat negative self-talk. Take heart, my friend; 2 Corinthians 4:16 reminds us, "Therefore we do not lose heart. Though outwardly we are wasting away, yet inwardly we are being renewed day by day."

When I took the time to honor and worship God in private, I felt most empowered when trouble was all around me. I acquired internal peace in a pause that stabilized me, but I had to slow down my mind, and will regardless of the chaos. There is assurance in knowing that he will perform his portion of the covenant if we do our part to pause.

SEIZE THE MOMENT

People ask how I find private relationship-building time with the Lord outside of public religious services. I smile and say I cannot afford not to. It is the only way to stay connected to God, who knows all—he is the source of direction and protection for our life. Time with God is not only an honor, but there is joy, peace, and a sense of great love experienced in God's presence. Just as God expresses affection toward me, I return it to him in praise and worship during moments of stillness. Those blocks of time in my day when I unplug from distractions and work assignments allow me to connect with God.

There have been too many times I have struggled with challenges all day, when at the end of the day I realized I had not acknowledged God and was doing it on my own. It's moments like those that an appreciation for depending on God as the source of successful living become clear. If you have been doing life on your own without interaction with and guidance from the Father, this is the time to stop and apologize in repentance for trying to manage your day on your own accord. I have had many days of stopping anywhere in my day to reach for my Bible and journal to read, pray, reflect, and worship.

The key to preserving good insight and preventing falling into a self-sufficiency trap is to learn how to implement modalities of pause into your day. Psalm 37:7 says, "Be still before the LORD and wait patiently for him." This is a source to resist daily stressful situations, to rediscover spiritual homeostasis, gain clarity of life, and to allow God to protect you from trouble. Seize the moment in a quiet space for three to five minutes. To begin you may not have much time, but as you choose to stop motion, sit in the quiet, relax, talk to God, and recite his promises, you will glean new perspectives and physical refreshing.

The devil always attempts to immobilize your efforts as you set out to pursue God's best for your life. But you must take action and use your moments of pause in faith to strengthen yourself as you step out and pursue your goals. Often, we have visions and goals and are overwhelmed of the expectations, but a little becomes much when we place it in the Master's hand. Ask him for directions.

Isaiah 30:15 reminds us that "in quietness and trust is your strength." Remember that it is "not by might, nor by power, but by my Spirit, says the LORD Almighty" (Zechariah 4:6). It takes only a small amount of faith to step out in the quietness of his confidence. As you do, you will be strengthened to pursue a deeper relationship with God and answer his call.

To hear from God during your quiet times, your mind should be cleared from the clutter of life. You have to learn to say no to some engagements, stop ruminating over plans, and learn to let God work out issues in his time and keep your hands off the situation. I said to myself, "Relax and rest. God has showered you with blessings. Soul, you've been rescued from death; Eye, you've been rescued from tears; and you, Foot, were kept from stumbling" (Psalm 116:7-8 MSG). Set some time aside to make your mind available for God's leading and creative guidance. Your mind's availability and alertness to God's presence allows for clarity of new ideas, directions, and solutions for any challenge.

The more time you spend in God's presence, the more like him you will become. It will also be easier to distinguish your thoughts from his voice. Your soul becomes cleansed, enabling you to live a life of wholeness as you apply the Scriptures daily. Beloved, understand that although you may be skilled and knowledgeable enough to handle the job at hand, the greater assurance is in knowing how to use Scripture in spiritual battle to release the power of God's spirit. The idea is to reset your focus on God. The touch of his love stimulates calmness and confidence in God. This safe place allows you to rest and relax as you continue to trust the Lord as your provider and protector.

MANAGING YOUR DREAM AND GOD'S PLAN

We all want to achieve goals, obtain promotions, and be in the will of God. The hustle and bustle that comes with competition can drain hope, replacing it with fear and doubt. The more we encounter God privately, our trust increases as peace and hope are replenished. Juggling the demands of society to be productive can take a lot of time, sleepless nights, and much frustration. Seeking to clearly understand the will of God for our life begins when we focus on eternal things. The apostle Paul said it perfectly, to set our thoughts on things in heaven, not earthly things (Colossians 3:2). Too often, we have no time for God to explore his direction for our life's purpose. When we avoid pausing, it leads to running in many directions until we finally uncover our life's call. The exhaustion of living a dual life to please self and God can lead to an imbalance, with poor health and spiritual destitution.

One of the significant acts of pause is surrendering our time and will to obey Scripture and follow the Holy Spirit's leading. Many times I felt like I was wrestling with myself, in "self versus self," only to find out that God was trying to tell me something. I was wrestling un-surrendered to his will, and life was typically a hard struggle during those times. My pursuit of what I thought was my purpose was fragmented and created unnecessary extra time for networking and planning. There was limited sleep, headaches, negative thoughts of progress, and no joy. When I redirected my whole heart to God to hear what he wanted me to do, the situation changed for the better. However, as you know, human drive can often guide us in the opposite direction of purpose.

▌▌ PAUSE ON PURPOSE 10

DIVINE SUCCESS

*The LORD will send a blessing on your barns and on everything
you put your hand to. The LORD your God will bless you
in the land he is giving you.* – DEUTERONOMY 28:8

Have you ever watched the *Let's Make a Deal* game show? The prizes were exceptional—everything you wanted waited behind doors one, two, or three. To distract you, the host would offer an envelope that you assume had a large sum of money, which only complicated matters. The contestant would become confused and desire to choose one of the doors, only to get a dud—the prize no one wanted.

In my lifetime, many great opportunities I had prayed for came my way. When I failed to acknowledge the Lord for guidance in decision-making, I accepted what I thought was the best opportunity—only to discover it would be a rough journey, not God's best for me. What price will we pay for poor decisions, actions, or eliminating God from the plan? Bible teacher Kay Arthur says, "Make God's will the focus of your life day by day. If you seek to please him and him alone, you'll find yourself satisfied with life."[2]

Women like you and me are answering his call successfully in many areas of society. God desires to answer prayer, "blessing your house and everything you put your hand to." He is waiting for you. Lydia, a businesswoman, honored the Lord with her life in Acts 16:13-14. Let her example challenge you as a businesswoman, housewife, teacher, lawyer, doctor, or whatever your call; God wants you to succeed in your life efforts.

The blessing of God can begin today as you find yourself in Scripture, becoming strong and courageous. It can start today as you read, reflect, and pray for a renewed relationship with God in his presence. Whatever concerns you on this journey, submit it to God and wait for a guided answer for your success.

Reflection: Are you willing to exchange your busy schedule for time with God for divine direction, protection, and provision? He is waiting on you to bless, keep, and make his face shine on you.

Prayer: *Lord, enlighten me to the truth. As you reveal yourself, help me deny myself and follow you. Thank you for waiting patiently for me.*

11

SELF-CARE BEGINS WITH SPIRITUAL INTIMACY

*Don't you know that you yourselves are God's temple
and that God's Spirit dwells in your midst?*

1 CORINTHIANS 3:16

GROWING UP IN A CHRISTIAN TRADITION of women working in the home, church, and community and with careers, I saw them in constant motion. When did they sleep? I did not hear them saying, "I am going to the gym," nor did I see them taking breaks for a walk. Although they were devout to God and had a call on their lives, the stress placed on their bodies was ignored. Even as a child, I wondered why God did not remind them to care for their bodies. There seemed to be the idea that God would take care of them as long as they took care of his business, that God was only concerned with constant doing and not rest. They had great faith and hope in God, but many ignored their health until they deteriorated physically and mentally. They were ignoring the signals of burnout.

Another term for burnout is *allostatic load*. It is the unrecognized demands on the entire body—the brain and physiological composition. Women who neglect self-care are unconscious of chronic stress as the tasks they are assigned consistently fall like a stack of dominoes. Allostatic load uncorrected can lead to diagnoses of diseases that can be circumvented when listening to God in prayer and stillness.

A lot of chatter is going on about self-care. There are books, podcasts, blogs, you name it, on the topic of self-care. All the resources can be daunting, coupled with the time needs of work and home life, leaving no room for self-care. Whenever I present at a women's retreat, conference, or day of guided solitude, we begin with an assessment of daily energy expended. Why? Identifying where we use our energy is a way of evaluating when, where, and what time is spent on. This is an open door to a simple way of beginning self-care of the spirit, mind, and body. There is an energy audit in appendix A for you to complete. Spiritual care in daily private time with God is the launching pad for a better you, when you listen and obey the leading of the Holy Spirit for your total well-being. Spiritual intimacy is the root to successful living.

As we look further at why and how intimacy results in wholeness, we discover that women who find time in their day to practice spiritual development are at peace. They have learned to pace themselves, to maintain focus, and to counteract chronic stress loads. Those who choose to retreat from the speed of life learn that spirituality can be a remedy to avoid burnout and heal mind and body. Educator and author Parker Palmer wrote, "Burnout is a state of emptiness, to be sure, but it does not result from giving all I have: it merely reveals the nothingness from which I was trying to give in the first place."[1] The practice of pause redirects dependence on God for everything—we remember to focus on the sufficiency of his grace.

Today, not much has changed in terms of church women being the primary volunteer staff for the operation of the ministry; thus, pausing to care consistently for our temples, in most cases, is on the back burner. We can obey God in some areas and be disobedient in our bodies' emotional and physical care. Pressing pause will aid us in assessing the needs of our bodily temple daily if we are attentive and willing to be obedient to do those necessary things for total temple care. For example, quality rest, balanced meals, recreational time, social and family time, and times of solitude. If we are not careful to slow down long enough to be mindful of our mental and physical health, it will be neglected. Just as our homes, churches, and cars need maintenance for preventive care, so do our bodies.

THE HOLDING GAME

Near the end of the first half of a workday, I realized I had not taken the bathroom break I had promised myself I would take almost two hours prior. Sitting twisting, bearing down, and crossing my legs, I could not hold it any longer and ran down the hall for relief. Sitting there, I thought to myself *This is abuse; it is damaging my bladder and is unnecessary*. Later that day, I wondered how often women came into the office with urinary incontinence, urinary tract infection, cystitis, and other health issues that occur when physical homeostasis for the renal system is imbalanced and uncorrected. The urge to urinate is designed to empty waste from our body, and as you see, I ignored the alarm. What about you? How often do you ignore the signal in your body to take a break and care for your temple? Alarms for emotional and mental rest ring, too. Do you ignore the alarms? As servant leaders in any capacity, caring for our bodies matters both spiritually and physically. First Timothy 4:8 says, "For physical training is of some value, but godliness has value for all things, holding promise for both the present life and the life to come."

Balanced living doesn't mean all parts are equal, but that each aspect of our body is being cared for as a total woman. Effectiveness is most achievable when one understands the importance of spiritual well-being as the foundation of being healthy in spirit, mind, and body. With prompting from the Holy Spirit, each temple component can be aligned and operate in harmony.

FIVE KEY SELF-CARE STARTERS

Not every fad diet and self-care strategy is appropriate for everyone. Learning the basics and building knowledge from other's experience empowers our decisions and protects our spirit, mind, and body. Here are five self-care starters that you can choose from to restore your temple.

1. Assess your stress.

   - Use the tool in appendix A to assess where your time and energy is spent.

   - Know your why with a personality assessment, such as the one in appendix B.

   - Determine the quality of your nutrition in your meals and beverages.

   - Evaluate how many times a week you exercise.

2. Avoid stressful situations.

   - Establish age-appropriate primary care and meet with a counselor.

   - Practice tools discussed in counseling to maintain boundaries.

   - Find an accountability partner to call and aid with decisions or actionable items.

   - Take monthly sabbaticals of rest (try a museum, hotel stay, massage, or long drive).

3. Adjust your mindset.

   - See yourself as God does, *whole*—execute the behavioral change and live as God sees you.

   - Practice positive self-talk and break ties with toxic relationships.

   - Practice what you learn in counseling to prevent responses to triggers of old habits.

4. Activate new lifestyle modifications, new behaviors.

- Develop or revisit a self-care plan weekly (utilize the template in appendix C).

- Insist that others respect boundaries you set in place to maintain your peace.

- Locate healthy emotional surroundings for a pause at your workplace.

- Exercise per age tolerance. (Stretching is suitable for any age.)

5. Apply new information gleaned in this book.

- Read chapter twelve on the fundamentals of quiet time.

- Continue spiritual growth (such as in part three of the seven-day personal retreat).

- Remind yourself that balanced living is not equal parts.

- Adjust physical activity and diet changes slowly with a physical trainer and nutritionist.

In chapter twelve you will be prepared further in the fundamentals of quiet time to execute a seven-day personal retreat. This is designed to continue developing skills for spiritual rest in the presence of God in quiet as you learn to align spirit, mind. and body.

PAUSE ON PURPOSE 11

STEP INTO THE LIGHT

You, LORD, keep my lamp burning;
my God turns my darkness into light. — PSALM 18:28

In the dark, I was trying to find a flashlight or candles after a tornado caused a power outage. Moving around the room, I paused to determine whether I was near a set of stairs, a door, or even a window to gain my bearings in the pitch black. Finally, reaching the laundry room, I moved my arm across the washing machine to grab a flashlight off the shelf. Yay! I found one, but no batteries were in it. It became necessary to go downstairs, because I knew there were candles and matches there. Gliding my hand on the walls, I found the banister and let it guide me to the last step, then the kitchen floor. It was with joy I found the matches in the first draw I checked and a candle nearby on the countertop.

Finding the light to proceed toward goals and dreams is necessary. This is what occurs when we pause for time with God. Too often, in pursuit of purpose, the refusal to slow down actually impedes progress because of active comparison or fear that we will not reach the mark. In order for me to have light after the storm, I had to step into the darkness. Obedience to God in a world that seems to offer everything challenges us to trust God to enable us to successfully complete our task. Pause more often and hold on to the walls of the heart of God, and he will lead you to the light victoriously every time.

Pause is a tool for spiritual growth. It is what keeps us motivated and focused as we move peacefully toward the prize. Psalm 27:1 says, "The LORD is my light and my salvation—whom shall I fear?"

Reflection: We all carry a light of hope for others. Whose light are you following? The Light of the World is waiting . . . pause and come away into his guiding light.

Prayer: Lord, you see me. I sense your presence even when life is dark. Help me trust in you rather than men, societal trends, and my own will. Father, I want to know you. Amen.

12

FUNDAMENTALS
FOR QUIET TIMES

Now if I have indeed found favor in Your sight,
please teach me Your ways, and I will know
You and find favor in Your sight.

Exodus 33:13 HCSB

On this quest to teach the personal practices of pausing in various ways for spiritual maturity, I have grown to enjoy the method of soaking in God's presence in silent periods of pause. These practices reset spiritual homeostasis in the life of anyone who wants spiritual wholeness. Healthy spirituality requires active interaction and a commitment to honor time scheduled for God in private.

Quiet time is important to God, but it should also be important to us. Our fellowship with the Father will also positively affect others. Developing a personal relationship with God during quiet time helps to nurture and discipline us, and it prepares us for fellowship and evangelism as we develop spiritual gifts to fulfill our God-given purpose. It is also a key to helping us make wise choices in our daily lives.

As women, access to serenity gained from disciplining ourselves in these methods of pause eliminates doubt and anxiety that lead to a sense of hopelessness. It is a prerequisite to find space and time to unwind and reconnect with God for effectiveness. Maintaining spiritual homeostasis is the answer for allostatic load stress, which is the cumulative effect of chronic stress.

Chronic stress is back-to-back tension, from good or bad situations without relief. We carry life loads in many forms for days, weeks, months, and years of consistent demands that wear and tear on the body. Can you imagine the trauma? The practice of pause enables us to strip the lingering impact from our spirits as it resets the mind and body to operate in the perfection it was created to function. It doesn't happen automatically; we have to do the work of finding time, by incorporating in our schedule the action of submission to align with God. He will direct our self-care of spirit, which enlightens our awareness before those in church or the marketplace.

To be most effective as women moving at the speed of light to meet the demands of the world, a guaranteed plan must be time-honored. As you progress through the seven-day retreat, you will begin with the fundamentals of quiet time methods of pause and sample small morsels of self-care implementation tips to begin synchronizing the balance of spirit, mind, and body.

One of the main goals for meeting God each day is to become more spiritually mature by examining and modeling the character of God in the world. The only way to obtain spiritual maturity is by communicating each day with God through his Word and prayer. Christians who maintain quality quiet time almost without exception have an effective witness experience each day. This is evident in the life of Christ: Jesus consistently had a positive effect on the people he met because he met with God before he met with the people. There were also occasions he was confronted with conflict, but he used the Scriptures to mediate a solution.

Throughout this book, you have read about various versions, names, and examples of quiet time to be certain you gain an understanding that there are many names that mean the same thing. To press pause simply means an act of surrender of time, sitting with the Father, but it can be challenging to submit to it wholeheartedly.

COMPONENTS OF AN EFFECTIVE QUIET TIME

Quiet time is the foundation upon which we build a deeper relationship with God. That is why we must make the most of the time we spend in his presence. The following are some of the elements we can include.

Make a plan. Know when, where, and how long your quiet time pause will be and what approach you will use. The key to a successful quiet time is to determine the location of this meeting of the heart. It should be permanent so that you can leave your materials there and not have to hunt them down every day, which results in missed appointments with God.

Again, this appointment can be during the morning, afternoon, or evening. You have to decide when it is best for you. The example Christ practiced suggests that you should have a quiet time in the morning because it sets the tone for you to enter your day refreshed, confident, with affirmations to reflect on in moments of pause throughout the day. Literally make an appointment in your calendar. Try to commit to at least fifteen or thirty minutes, but you can adjust the timeframe as needed. The key is to do what is best for you until you become disciplined in this process.

Pray. Ask God for focus and understanding so you may receive what he is speaking to you, both through his written Word and to your spirit. I often encourage those who don't know what to do during their quiet time to use the following to help guide their prayers. Appendix D also includes a prayer guide you can utilize.

1. Begin with thanksgiving. This is the act of saying, "Thank you, Lord." Think about all your blessings (food, clothes, shelter, protection).

2. Confess your sins and consecrate yourself to God. This is when you can repent for any disobedient actions or thoughts, whether intentional or unintentional.

3. Intercede for others. This encourages you to release and join your faith with others to see God manifest his power in and for others. The intercessory prayer takes your mind off your own needs.

4. Petition for yourself. These can be spoken or unspoken requests, needs, or desires. Questions also are acceptable.

5. Give God adoration and praise. You do this as you honor God for who he is and for his divine ability to bless you above and beyond your wildest hopes and dreams.

I also have found it helpful to play praise and worship music to help set the atmosphere and prepare my heart for a visitation of the Holy Spirit. (See appendix E for playlists.) Listening to praise and worship music helps me move beyond the veil of my flesh into his presence.

Do not let the elements of prayer frighten you. Many people worry that they may not be saying the right things in prayer, or not saying them in the right way. But there is not just one right way to pray.

You can go through the previously mentioned elements. Or you can read or recite the Lord's Prayer (Matthew 6:9-13). It is called the model prayer because it includes all the elements needed for effective prayer. Even if you only pray one sentence from your heart, God honors it.

Prayer is a form of communication from our heart and mind to God. It can be vocal or silent. It is like having an internal telephone.

Read the Bible. If you are studying a prepared lesson from a book or notes from a sermon or church service, practice reading the selected Bible passage twice. You might have to write the passage or a particular verse down verbatim or read it aloud a few times to provide additional clarity. Repetition will reinforce the Scripture and allow it to penetrate your spirit.

If possible, purchase a Bible with a concordance. It helps you to locate additional words and Scripture references to help you build a database of positive affirmations and confessions for every area of concern that occurs.

Keep a journal. Transfer the truths that God reveals to you down onto paper. If using a study guide, answer the questions at the end of the lesson in your journal. If you have not selected a guide, record and review Sunday's sermon or Bible study notes in a notebook or journal. Write your favorite Scriptures down and apply them to your situations and circumstances. Make the effort to memorize Scriptures you may have written down. For example, you might want to memorize Psalm 119:11, which says, "I have hidden your word in my heart that I might not sin against you." The more Scripture verses you learn and recite (silently or vocally), the more your faith will be increased. See appendix F for a Scripture bank.

Reflect or meditate on Scripture. Take time to think about what God has taught you through his Word, as Psalm 1:2 says: "But his delight is in the law of the LORD; and in his law doth he meditate day and night" (KJV). Meditate by seeing or imagining yourself in the Scripture verse or passage. Take ownership of its promises, and confess by faith what you believe God is doing for you.

Incorporating these elements will allow you to have an effective quiet time, grow spiritually, and take on the characteristics of God. J. I. Packer said it this way: "The world's greatest need is the personal holiness of Christian people."[1]

HINDRANCES TO EFFECTIVE QUIET TIME

Recognizing hindrances is critical to our spiritual growth. Hindrances are a weapon the enemy will use to try to steal time from God's presence. Delays and hindrances to a deeper relationship, spiritual maturity, and favor with God and man include: distractions from Satan, laziness or procrastination, fatigue due to schedule overload, discouragement, and lack of a suitable location.

These hindrances can be overcome by being honest with yourself about how you are preparing for your meeting time with God. Ask yourself: Did I put any thought into preparing an agenda? Did you put the same effort into preparing for the presence of the Holy Spirit as you did to welcome a special friend into your home? What might be some hindrances or excuses that you face? These are some common excuses that can enter your thoughts—don't yield to them.

This could include saying any of the following:

- I do not know how to study the Bible.
- I am not good at praying.
- I have no privacy in my house.
- I cannot get up early in the morning.
- I don't have time; my schedule is too full.
- I can't concentrate.

In any case, don't allow hindrances or excuses to prevent you from following through with the scheduled time agreement for spiritual growth.

PAUSE MODELS: SOLITUDE AND SOAKING

There are many ways to increase your spiritual connection with God for direction and answers when in your space of prayer and calm waiting on God. You save time and energy from stumbling around mishaps. Listed below are two methods to exercise, and you can determine which one best fits your time as you learn to wait in quiet spaces with him.

Solitude. We read earlier about an example by Jesus that can be used by new or seasoned Christians: "Very early in the morning, while it was still dark, Jesus got up, left the house and went off to a solitary place, where he prayed" (Mark 1:35). In this verse, we find a pattern for quiet time that we can use even today.

1. Jesus arose early.
2. Jesus left the house (his sleeping area).
3. Jesus went to a solitary place.
4. Jesus prayed.

This verse is showing us an ideal schedule early in the morning: arising, leaving our beds, and going somewhere quiet to pray and devote time to God. Jesus' pattern reveals two major components of successful moments of pause:

- *Time*—When we meet with God early, our mind is fresh and our heart is quiet.
- *Atmosphere*—We meet with God in isolated stillness, without distractions and noise.

The value of pausing teaches us how to wait constructively with grace. When my children were small, I started coloring in adult coloring books and listening to worship music, which can always be added to quiet time. It was a time to rest my mind after time with the Lord and before moving to the next item on my schedule.

Soaking (sacred stillness). Lying on the floor before the Lord in complete surrender has become one of my favorite forms of pause as an act of true silence that leads to worship. There is an acronym, *S.O.A.K.,* that I like using for this method of pause. It is the sacred stillness of observation, absorption of power, and koinonia with God. In this posture of pause, I yield totally with laying down of arms to embrace his essence. All motion stops, time recedes, and the mental door to all distractions is blocked during this expression of reflective transformation.

We begin soaking by sitting or lying down quietly, meditating on Scripture truths without any noise, listening to our bodies as we take a few deep breaths. If we are near a window or outside, we observe nature; we might have a special touchstone to hold. As we continue reflecting, we sense God's presence filling the room. We invite him to sit with us in thanksgiving, adoration, and honor.

When you soak, you can praise him for his goodness and mighty acts. Rest and listen, read your Bible, and glean inner peace and confirmation, knowing that God loves you and will perform his Word. You might stand, walk, raise your hands as you enter a new level of worship, or turn on worship music to your liking.

The calm of his embodiment relaxes your awareness as you reposition, lying or sitting down. Prepare to listen; God will soothe you to impart wisdom and knowledge, and direction into your heart. I've shared my song playlist in appendix E to stimulate an atmosphere of gratitude and worship. Let your spiritual senses reveal to you visions, dreams, and instructions. Keep a pen and journal handy to write it down. (Some people record these moments and later transcribe.) During this time of pause, you don't want to rush in and out as the power of God is being poured out. This is why it is necessary to prepare a place to meet God with supplies. Soaking is usually planned as extended time in the morning or evening.

Showing up as scheduled consistently will pay off as you see the benefits of maintaining a healthy spiritual connection with the Father, who will illuminate your path. In your practice of soaking, learn to wait patiently for the Lord's prompting to know how and when to move to the next step. J. I. Packer once said, "When in doubt, do nothing, but continue to wait on God. When action is needed, light will come."[2]

A SEVEN-DAY RETREAT

Join other readers like you on a specially designed seven-day personal retreat to implement what you have read and learned in this book. If you need accountability and fellowship, there is a private Facebook group. If you are already a friend of mine on my page, Karynthia Phillips, you will be allowed into the group. You will then have access to my song playlist to incite an atmosphere of gratitude and worship.

MY PRAYER FOR YOU

Lord, I thank you for this reader because you have made them godly and free. Even in temptation and failure, you are able to lift their head and keep them saved through the delivering power of your Word. I thank you for removing the pain of their youth and adult life. Today, they walk in joy. You have forgiven their past and made it beautiful, as they walk into the future. I know all things work together for good. They will be led by you, Lord, as you teach them to use past experiences to heal other broken hearts, as you have done for me. Amen.

Part 3

DARE TO GROW

A Seven-Day Personal Retreat

I miss sitting with you, God, in our room,
just me and my Father in the absence
of time, when we intimately gather . . .

LILIANA KOHANN

INTRODUCTION

HAS YOUR LIFE EVER BEEN so fragmented that you felt like Humpty Dumpty, who had a great fall off a wall? They could not put Humpty Dumpty back together again. The nursery rhyme suggests the probability that he had fallen and had been repaired before; however, this time, they could not put him back together again. Are you burned out, overwhelmed, or feeling broken? There is good news: You can be restored, refreshed, and renewed. Look over your schedule and find a week that you can commit in quiet communion connecting with our Father.

After choosing a date and starting the seven-day retreat, you will journey toward a total you in the quietness of pause. In these spaces of time, you will connect with God. If you are willing to find time to unplug and reconnect with yourself and God, there will be a fresh surge experienced in your meetups. In these seven days, wake up every morning and practice pause, guided by the format in the following pages.

As you work through each day of the personal retreat, questions are available to answer to help you focus. In stillness, you will learn to jot down thoughts in your journal and excitedly return your focus on engaging with God. You will have time to process how the Scripture passage might apply, enlighten, or bring an answer in your current situation. As you continue growing in the presence of the Holy Spirit, you will explore other Scriptures that resonate with you naturally and spontaneously. Your faith and trust in partnership with God will become easier as you find peace with every step you take toward your purpose. You will learn to watch the hand of God move in your life and in others who face critical decision-making, adversity, promotions, health, sickness, death, and other life events. Your confidence and hope in God will increase as you appreciate the value of time spent in fellowship and developing companionship with him.

Below are lists to set up your retreat in advance, including planned bedtime practices and needed materials. In preparation, keep in mind that consistency of time in the morning also includes planned bedtime practices.

1. Set an alarm on your phone to stop working, watching TV, or reading to prepare for bed.

2. Relax and remove stimulating devices and materials from the bedroom so you have a clean sleep area.

3. Prepare for sleep by keeping affirmations, prayer, and journaling options near the bed.

4. Determine beforehand where you will sit during your morning retreat time.

5. Review your self-care plan each morning to enforce your decision to pause.

What are some habits you want to discontinue for better sleep to wake refreshed?

Materials for this personal retreat:

1. The seven brief devotionals included here, with prompts to assist with prayer, reflection, and self-care.

2. The private Facebook group to engage in the experience with others on this retreat.

3. A time and place for meeting God with supplies accessible.

4. A writing instrument and a journal.

5. A Bible translation of your choice.

6. A playlist of music (avoid yielding to scroll if you use your phone).

The night before starting the retreat, spend time in worship and thanksgiving, sit still in expectation of his presence. Read the following Scripture as a prayer:

Teach me, LORD, the way of your decrees,
that I may follow it to the end.
Give me understanding, so that I may keep your law
and obey it with all my heart.
Direct me in the path of your commands,
for there I find delight.
Turn my heart toward your statutes
and not toward selfish gain.
Turn my eyes away from worthless things;
preserve my life according to your word.
Fulfill your promise to your servant,
so that you may be feared.
Take away the disgrace I dread,
for your laws are good.
How I long for your precepts!
In your righteousness preserve my life. (Psalm 119:33-40)

See yourself sitting with God, talking with him as you enter the act of meditation on the passage. Allow hunger to increase to know God—the Word. Underline or circle the word(s) or phrase(s) that add light to your decision to find time daily with him.

Reflection: Unplugging from the cares of life to connect with God slows your spirit, mind, and body down to regain homeostasis—wholeness.

Prayer: Lord we entrust the readers to you on this spiritual exploration. Guide each of them as they dive deep in your Word, touch their ears, eyes, and nose to sense your presence in a tangible way. Thank you for doing a new work in their lives.

Day 1

HIS LOVE IS WAITING

*Because of the Lord's great love we are not
consumed, for his compassions never fail.*

Lamentations 3:22

I have been there, when I would wake up sluggish in the morning. Then count, one, two, three, I am up and out of bed. Quickly saying, "Lord, I thank you for waking me up," letting the dog out, getting dressed, making coffee, scrolling social media, and out the door. Days of this behavior to join the millions in the game of life and productivity. After several days to weeks of this, I would begin to long for something. What was missing? God's embrace, feeling guilty for ignoring his presence.

The better way to start my day, I have learned, is to choose an intentional time to wake up and go to a prepared, calm space for prayer, Scripture reading, journaling, and biblical affirmation. It has been the source of managing my attitude for my day. The act of practicing quiet time with God has enhanced my memory and overall physical and mental health. Awareness begins when acknowledging and accepting the invitation into a relationship filled with love and mercy. He is waiting, arms open with love.

Spiritual saturation in the morning assures that we ground ourselves with truth before the day is filled with chaos. Morning stillness helps us manage our attitudes throughout the day. This habit of intimacy with God boosts a rhythm of consistent balance in our lives. I don't always make the mark, and you will not either, but he loves us, and his mercies are new every morning.

REFLECTION AND JOURNALING

How can you extend grace and mercy to yourself to start your day with God every morning?

_____

_____

_____

_____

_____

TEMPLE CARE

Today what will you do to refresh your mind or body?

_____

_____

_____

_____

_____

_____

PRAYER

Help me, Lord, to honor your presence and guide me throughout the day.

Day 2

POSITIVE CONNECTIVITY

So that your faith might not rest on human wisdom,
but on God's power.

1 Corinthians 2:5

Our faithful printer finally gave up the ghost and died. We purchased a new one and found that it was not as faithful to the Wi-Fi connection. Each time we attempted to print a document, the software had to be reinstalled and reconnected to the Wi-Fi via a cable to fully reconnect.

The Wi-Fi network is like a symbol of relationships between people. All who have the password have access to the internet filled with knowledge and power to succeed at any task. This same idea corresponds to a Christian's relationship with God. Think about the vastness of the characteristics he possesses—omnipresent, omniscient, and omnipotent, better than the internet!

Connection with God guarantees that he sees us, that we are heard, that we are valued, and that we can be unaffected by a sense of false judgment. A Christian's relationship with God is provisional for sustainability and lasting fruitfulness in life. Finding time to pause prevents faltering connections, so that we build trust to rest our faith in God and his power and not the ideologies of man's wisdom.

What are the challenges that are stopping you from unplugging to reconnect with God? In your daily routine, you might have to decide what is more important as the source of strength and vision to pursue your goals and dreams.

REFLECTION AND JOURNALING

What commitment to God will assist you in connecting with him more?

_____

_____

_____

_____

_____

TEMPLE CARE

Today what will you do to refresh your mind or body?

_____

_____

_____

_____

_____

PRAYER

Father, as I unplug to pause and reconnect with your power and love, help me download strength and wisdom for this day.

Day 3

NETWORKING MEETUPS

Those who know your name trust in you, for you, LORD,
have never forsaken those who seek you.

PSALM 9:10

I PUT COMMUNITY MEETINGS IN my planner and my electronic calendar. I don't want to miss a writing meetup, healthcare networking opportunity, or church leadership meeting. Those gatherings provide wholesome opportunities to grow and thrive toward goals, as I learn members' names and what their expertise is. I begin to form bonds of trust for work relationships. Rarely missing a meeting, even when exhausted, these standing meetings are never substituted with another event, because of the value to me in pursuing my goals.

Meeting in quiet places with God is as important as the pursuit to make those meetings to gain worth and increase productivity. But we can find there is a sure way to "work smarter not harder," trusting the Lord to never forsake those who seek him first.

The projects I was on that flopped are those that I did not consult with God about. Ninety-nine percent of the time, the failure is because I did not acknowledge God in prayer, nor did I pursue him for direction. Have you ever experienced regret for doing your own thing? Making room to develop a relationship with God is more beneficial than those nurtured at the meetups. His expertise and guidance can always be trusted by those who inquire of him.

Doing life has become easier as I intentionally lean in with a trusting heart to listen for his instructions. When was the last time you paused long enough to talk with God about your projects, job, or overall mission in life?

REFLECTION AND JOURNALING

How can you streamline your schedule to meet with God at the table of wisdom and knowledge for direction?

_____

_____

_____

_____

TEMPLE CARE

Today what will you do to refresh your mind or body?

_____

_____

_____

_____

PRAYER

Lord, I want to know you. Guide me each day to seek you first to answer the call for my life.

Day 4

OUR DAILY BREAD

*For the bread of God is the bread that comes down
from heaven and gives life to the world.*

JOHN 6:33

EVEN MY BETTA FISH, Big Blue, knows to come to the top of his fishbowl when he senses I am in the room. Breaking away from his routine of bottom searching, swimming around decorative ornaments, or gazing out of the glass, straight to the top he swims to nibble on the small crumbs of food.

Over the past two decades, society has become exhausted, reminding the body of the need for food, the spirit for inspiration, the soul for tending, and the mind for fresh creativity. Finding time has become less important, although the chaos increases. I often think about the old way and returning to the basics. It is when I come up for air, like Big Blue, out from the clutter of demands, that energy is renewed. I find strength from the peace of God's presence.

Most people eat at least one or two meals per day, feeding their bodies at home, during meetings, and in ministry activities. What about the needs of the spirit? The busyness in our lives might be leading to success, but how much is it worth to starve the core of our beings—our spirit? Today God has everything we need for life. During this pause, glean what you can, but you can come back later for more. Learn to feed your spirit throughout the day in reflection. It's like eating leftovers.

REFLECTION AND JOURNALING

What are some of the leftovers of God's presence that you've seen these last few days?

_____

_____

_____

_____

_____

_____

TEMPLE CARE

Today what will you do to refresh your mind or body?

_____

_____

_____

_____

_____

_____

PRAYER

Lord, refresh me this day as sprinkles of your presence fall upon me.

Day 5

THE PIED PIPER
RHYTHMS OF LIFE

You did not choose me, but I chose you and
appointed you so that you might go and bear fruit—
fruit that will last.

JOHN 15:16

TRAVELING ON LIFE'S JOURNEY as a Christian, there are many voices and opportunities that can sway us off the path of God's original plan for our lives. The rhythmic movement can increase our pace, speeding ahead of God—and there are times our pace decreases in a lagging motion, resulting in missing the mark. These ups and downs further distract, fatigue, and block our hearing the rhythmic voice of God. The whispers of chatter about new ideas and devices mute the call of God as we move in the opposite direction of his voice.

In your hurry, what rhythmic beat regulates your motion? What voices are you being enticed by? The Holy Spirit is near, calling, and waiting for you to come near to him. Can you hear his voice amid the other noise? Silence the others and accept his invitation to come.

In response to God's call, sit and be still to find rest for your soul. Keep your eyes on God and your ears open to his voice to dismiss the rhythmic distractions that pull you away from his love.

REFLECTION AND JOURNALING

What are you discovering about the leading of the Holy Spirit for daily direction?

_____

_____

_____

_____

_____

_____

_____

TEMPLE CARE

Today what will you do to refresh your mind or body?

_____

_____

_____

_____

_____

_____

_____

PRAYER

Lord, I want to know you. Help me become more attuned to your voice above all other voices.

Day 6

FILL MY CUP

Thou preparest a table before me in the presence of mine enemies:
thou anointest my head with oil; my cup runneth over.

PSALM 23:5 KJV

RUNNING ON NEAR EMPTY, my mind racing to the next task, wondering how I will make it. Would it be easier to drive up to a gas station and have my spiritual tank filled up? What about my favorite tea? I reach for it in hope of regaining strength. A consistent, healthy relationship with God provides access to him faster than brewing a hot beverage or filling up my gas tank.

The number of refills is limitless when we are positioned to receive the pouring of the Holy Spirit into our empty spirits. The nudge of spiritual thirst is an alarm that alerts us to a need for a refill of his power and love in his presence.

The benefits of finding time for God in moments of pause are like welcome sprinklings of his grace that strengthen and restore us as we bow at his feet. Our refills have been paid in full by Jesus' life, death, and resurrection. Ask the Holy Spirit to fill you up today. What joy and peace will ensue in the atmosphere, a presence that can hover for days.

Don't let your cup get too empty doing good, busy work that often ends with unfulfillment. A physical teacup is often fragile; so is your spirit when it has become depleted of God's presence.

God wants to fill you with his Spirit until he overflows blessings into your life and to everyone you are connected to. In your desire to be productive today, include space for him and watch your goals manifest as you pursue him and trust he will perform every promise.

REFLECTION AND JOURNALING

There is always a moment when you can pause and enjoy nature. Schedule a break today to refill your cup.

_____

_____

_____

_____

_____

_____

TEMPLE CARE

Today what will you do to refresh your mind or body?

_____

_____

_____

_____

_____

_____

PRAYER

Holy Spirit, I desire you to fill my cup with more of you.

Day 7

YOUR BEST YES

I desire to do your will, my God; your law is within my heart.

PSALM 40:8

INITIALLY, when I began serving in ministry, it was so easy to volunteer anytime I was asked to serve. This willingness continued into the marketplace and community service. There was nothing wrong with my commitment, but the time and distraction from the pursuit of purpose was prolonged. I have learned that asking God first about all I do aids me in giving my best yes to serve as unto God and directly to my divine purpose.

People pleasing can easily become a habit if we don't know when to say no. Also, when we don't take time to seek God's will concerning a matter, we may expend time on assignments that God has not ordained for us. This prolongs the manifestation of his perfect will in our life.

A personal relationship with God will mitigate many detours in life if we stick to the blueprint and listen for the leading of the Holy Spirit. When pressing into his presence, we become familiar with his voice and confident to communicate with him anywhere throughout the day.

You can be in a board meeting or at a parent-teacher consultation, and need help to accept or decline an offer. In the depths of your heart, you can quietly ask the Father, "Lord, what should I do?" In a pause, stop, look, and listen. He will answer. It is in the pressure of life we often forget the two-letter word *no*. Let your "No, not at this time" be your best yes to the plan of God for your life. The key to staying on course with your purpose begins by giving God your best yes.

REFLECTION AND JOURNALING

How can you pause daily to give your best yes?

_____

_____

_____

_____

_____

TEMPLE CARE

Today, what will you do to refresh your mind or body?

_____

_____

_____

_____

_____

PRAYER

Father, help me to courageously answer yes to you. It is my desire to continue spending time with you. Open my eyes to see clear the path that I am to take as I follow you.

ACKNOWLEDGMENTS

Pause is the integration of spirituality, and self-care is the prescription of life for all women.

The practice of pause in the posture of quiet is a spiritual discipline that has evolved over time as the protocol for self-preservation, for me and every woman like me, who often needs permission to extend grace to themselves and intentionally pause for no reason guilt-free, other than to tend to their spirit, mind, and body.

I am thankful for the guides as led by the Holy Spirit throughout this journey.

My first mentor, Virginia Hazel Armstrong Glasper, a woman of prayer and worship, the one who has always cheered me on from the sidelines.

I am thankful for my dad, James Edward Glasper, who believed I could do anything with his approving smile.

I am thankful for my spiritual parents and each of their congregations' support: Bishop Jonathan and Jessie Powell and Bishop Horace and Kiwanis Hockett, pastors emeritus, who have walked with me, praying for me through every project and book I have penned. This book is to remind me that giving up is not an option.

To the intercessors in my life. You know who you are . . . it would be impossible to name you all, so I pray the Holy Spirit brings to your remembrance every prayer you have prayed for me with unshakable faith. I love you all very much for always being available.

I am honored to have the supportive members of the Christian publishing industry in my life who have helped me along the way. Joyce Dinkins, a woman who has worn many hats in my life as editor, encourager, and guide. I have never heard a negative word out of her mouth, only a voice with a prophetic tone and skilled instructions to blossom in each published work. Her spiritual guidance called my gift to manifestation.

Lisa Crayton, a spirit-led coach and mentor who tells it like it is while in the trenches with you. Her skillset and patience are a godsend. Thank you for a heart that desires to see productivity, excellence, and lasting fruit from the inner core of every author. Thank you.

I am grateful for Edwina Perkins and Edie Melson, the dynamic duo who always have their hands on my back, pushing and praying me to the next level—thank you.

Books & Such Literary Management, my agent Barb Roose, and "Bookie" Janet McHenry, with humbleness of heart, thank you.

InterVarsity Press, words cannot describe your professionalism and patience represented in every department by your Christlike work ethics, thank you.

To the readers, thank you for purchasing this book. You are the reason God charged me to write this primer as a life-transforming resource for those seeking to unplug from the force of societal motion and pause to refine intimacy with God for spiritual growth and balanced living.

To my husband, Timothy Phillips, and family and friends, thank you for making space for me to write, rest, and write.

If I haven't mentioned your names and you have been there for me, encouraging, praying, and supporting in other ways, thank you.

We did it again; another book made it through the process from concept to print.

ENERGY ASSESSMENT FOR BALANCE[1]

This assessment is a tool to evaluate on which component of your temple you spend most of your energy (time). Take three to five minutes and mark the statements that are true for you now. Add the number of marks in each section after you complete the entire assessment.

PHYSICAL
I don't regularly get at least seven to eight hours of sleep, and I often wake up feeling tired.
I frequently skip breakfast, or I settle for something that isn't nutritious.
I don't work out enough (meaning cardiovascular training at least three times a week).
I don't take regular breaks during the day to truly renew and recharge, or I often eat lunch at my desk, if I eat it at all.
Section total

MENTAL
I have difficulty focusing on one thing at a time, and I am easily distracted during the day, especially by email.
I spend much of my day reacting to immediate crises and demands rather than focusing on activities with longer-term value and high leverage.
I don't take enough time for reflection, strategizing, and creative thinking.
I work in the evenings or on weekends, and I almost never take an email–free vacation.
Section total

EMOTIONAL	
	I frequently find myself feeling irritable, impatient, or anxious at work, especially when work is demanding.
	I don't have enough time with my family and loved ones, and when I'm with them, I'm not always really with them.
	I have too little time for the activities that I most deeply enjoy.
	I don't stop frequently enough to express my appreciation to others or to savor my accomplishments and blessings.
	Section total
SPIRITUAL	
	I don't spend enough time at work doing what I do best and enjoy most.
	There are significant gaps between what I say is most important to me in my life and how I actually allocate my time and energy.
	My decisions at work are more often influenced by external demands than by a strong, clear sense of my own purpose.
	I don't invest enough time and energy in making a positive difference to others or to the world.
	Section total

SCORING GUIDE				
Guide to section score		**Guide to overall score**		
0	Excellent energy management skills	0–3	Excellent energy management skills	
1	Good/reasonable energy management skills	4–6	Good/reasonable energy management skills	
2	Some energy management deficits	7–10	Some energy management deficits	
3	Poor energy management practices	11–16	Significant energy management risks	
4	Significant energy management risks			

Rank the four sections in order from most to least checks. The one with the greatest number of checks will require the most attention to create balanced living.

LINKED PERSONALITY QUIZ

The LINKED Personality Assessment, created by Linda Goldfarb and Linda Gilden, is designed to help you understand why you relate to people and tasks the way you do. When you're ready to take the assessment visit **https://bit.ly/3zTCN7N** or use the QR code below.

After you complete the assessment, be sure to complete the following steps before submitting your responses:

1. Add my name (Karynthia Phillips) as the person who sent you the link.

2. Enter your first and last name.

3. Provide an email address where you can receive your results with an explanation of your personality type. Your results will be coming from Karynthia Phillips at Beyondboundaryconsulting@gmail .com, so be sure to check your spam folder if you don't see the email shortly after submitting your responses.

To learn more about LINKED, visit https://LindaGoldfarb.com.

SELF-CARE ACTION PLAN[1]

If you have determined what area needs the most work (appendix A) and your personality type (appendix B), you can insert your results in this self-plan. It is a map to balance out your lifestyle. Pray to find a Scripture that you can recite daily to assist with spiritual self-care to strengthen you to care for your entire body. One of my favorites is Isaiah 58:11 in the NLT. You may also use the Scriptures in appendix F for daily confessions.

MIND
- Choose affirmations of the week.
- Start a creative hobby.
- Make an appointment with a counselor.
- List supportive Scriptures.

BODY
- Make appointment for a physical.
- Commit to an eight-minute morning workout.
- Meet with a meal prep or nutrition coach.
- Eat two to three fruits and veggies each day.
- Set aside time for stretching each evening.

Supportive People in My Life

I Want to Accomplish

SPIRIT
- Commit to QT. When? Where?
- Pray for an accountability partner.
- List supportive Scriptures.

Sample self-care action plan. For fillable version go to https://beyondboundaryconsulting.com/products.

GUIDED PRAYER TIME

Use this guide during the seven-day personal retreat or anytime you choose (see instructions following).

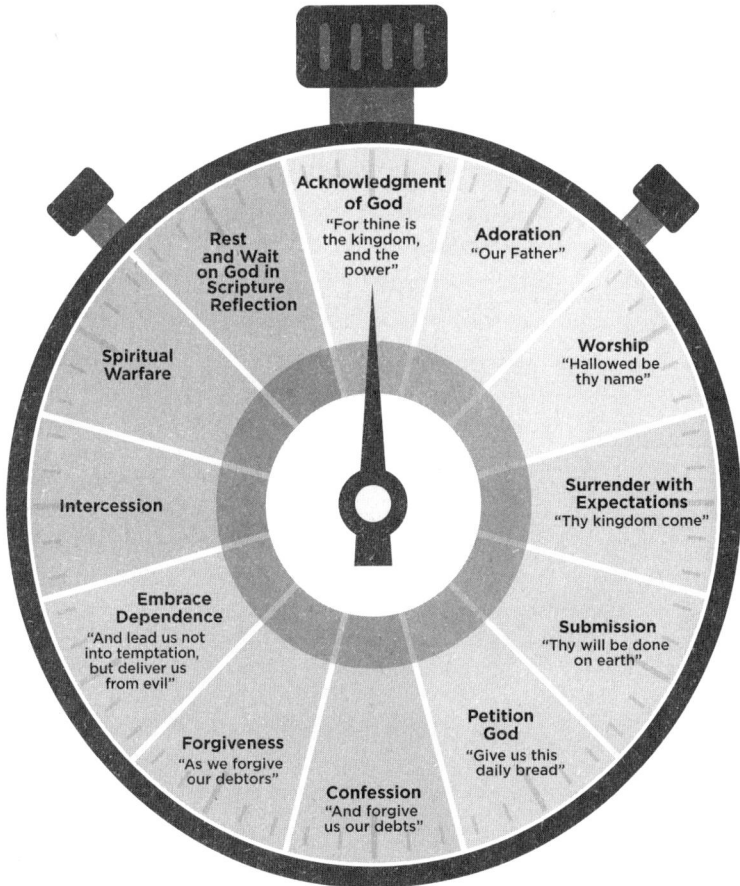

Acknowledgment of God
"For thine is the kingdom, and the power"

Adoration
"Our Father"

Worship
"Hallowed be thy name"

Rest and Wait on God in Scripture Reflection

Spiritual Warfare

Surrender with Expectations
"Thy kingdom come"

Intercession

Submission
"Thy will be done on earth"

Embrace Dependence
"And lead us not into temptation, but deliver us from evil"

Petition God
"Give us this daily bread"

Forgiveness
"As we forgive our debtors"

Confession
"And forgive us our debts"

You can pray for twelve minutes—one minute per item—or as short as thirty seconds per item.

Relax and rest as you embrace God's presence while reflecting on Scripture. In stillness, listen for God's voice audibly, through the Bible or as you journal. Take some deep breaths to clear your mind as you enter further into a posture of solitude for insightful journaling.

PERSONAL PLAYLISTS

These are songs I have compiled that I listen to before going into prayer and in times of soaking in the presence of God.

Press Pause: Making Room for God
in an Overscheduled Life

Soaking in His Gift
of Presence

Pause and Move with Him
Dancing with the Holy Spirit

SCRIPTURAL CONFESSIONS

It is important to memorize Scripture during our quiet times. Praying according to the Scriptures helps increase our faith. As you mature spiritually, you will increase your Scripture data bank and find yourself confessing God's Word daily, which will cause you to walk in victory. These scriptural confessions are quick resources to thumb through during the day for affirming declarations.

The following are Scripture passages you can meditate on each day.

PSALM 32:5-7 NKJV

I acknowledged my sin to You, and my iniquity I have not hidden. I said, "I will confess my transgressions to the Lord," And You forgave the iniquity of my sin. *Selah.*

For this cause everyone who is godly shall pray to You in a time when You may be found; Surely in a flood of great waters they shall not come near him. You are my hiding place; You shall preserve me from trouble; You shall surround me with songs of deliverance.

ACTS 24:16

I strive always to keep my conscience clear before God and man.

GALATIANS 1:10

Am I now trying to win the approval of human beings, or of God? Or am I trying to please people? If I were still trying to please people, I would not be a servant of Christ.

JAMES 5:16

Therefore confess your sins to each other and pray for each other so that you may be healed. The prayer of a righteous person is powerful and effective.

Confessing Healing

ISAIAH 61:3

Provide for those who grieve in Zion—
to bestow on them a crown of beauty
　　instead of ashes,
the oil of joy
　　instead of mourning,
and a garment of praise
　　instead of a spirit of despair.
They will be called oaks of righteousness,
　　a planting of the Lord
　　for the display of his splendor.

PSALM 107:20

He sent out his word and healed them;
　　he rescued them from the grave.

ISAIAH 61:1

The Spirit of the Sovereign Lord is on me,
because the Lord has anointed me
to proclaim good news to the poor.
He has sent me to bind up the brokenhearted.

Confessing a Commitment to Prayer

MARK 11:24

Therefore I tell you, whatever you ask for in prayer, believe that you have received it, and it will be yours.

ROMANS 12:12

Be joyful in hope, patient in affliction, faithful in prayer.

LUKE 5:16

But Jesus often withdrew to lonely places and prayed.

Confessing God's Will for Your Life

PROVERBS 21:5

The plans of the diligent lead to profit
  as surely as haste leads to poverty.

PROVERBS 16:3

Commit to the LORD whatever you do,
  and he will establish your plans.

Confessing the Truth

3 JOHN 1:2-4

Dear friend, I pray that you may enjoy good health and that all may go well with you, even as your soul is getting along well. It gave me great joy when some believers came and testified about your faithfulness to the truth, telling how you continue to walk in it. I have no greater joy than to hear that my children are walking in the truth.

Confessing Divine Peace

PSALM 94:19

When anxiety was great within me, your consolation brought me joy.

Confessing the Power of God's Word

JOSHUA 1:8

Keep this Book of the Law always on your lips; meditate on it day and night, so that you may be careful to do everything written in it. Then you will be prosperous and successful.

This Book of the Law shall not depart from my mouth, but I will meditate in it day and night, that I may observe to do according to all that is written in it: for then will You make my way prosperous and I will have good success.

Additional Confessions

The following fifty passages of Scripture are organized into common topics so you can easily reference passages during your quiet time that relate to specific challenges you may be facing.

THE CALL OF GOD

1. Romans 11:29
2. John 1:35-39
3. Deuteronomy 7:7-9
4. Luke 11:27-28
5. Psalm 85:8-9
6. 1 Corinthians 1:2-9
7. Jeremiah 1:4-10
8. Isaiah 6:1-9
9. Luke 9:28-36
10. Luke 11:27-28

LISTEN FOR GOD'S VOICE

11. Jeremiah 7:22-28

12. Deuteronomy 6:4-13

13. Isaiah 50:4-5

14. Hebrews 3:7-13

15. Jeremiah 7:1-11

LET GOD REVEAL HIMSELF TO YOU

16. Hosea 11:1-4

17. Titus 3:3-8

18. John 17:21-26

19. John 7:37-39

20. Mark 6:1-6

WALK BY FAITH AND WATCH THE INVISIBLE BECOME VISIBLE

21. Psalm 56

22. Psalm 125

23. James 1:2-18

24. Matthew 9:27-31

25. 1 Peter 5:6-11

PEACE AND CONFIDENCE FOR THE DAY

26. John 7:37

27. Isaiah 41:8-13

28. John 14:27-29

29. James 3:14-18

30. Psalm 52:8-9

SEEKING GOD

31. John 6:44-47

32. Psalm 73:23-28

33. Psalm 143:5-10

34. Psalm 105:1-5

35. 2 Chronicles 15:12-15

MAKING DECISIONS WITH TRUTH AND INTEGRITY

36. Matthew 15:1-20

37. Luke 6:43-45

38. Matthew 23:13-32

39. John 15:1-10

40. John 18:33-40

FINDING STRENGTH BEYOND YOURSELF

41. 1 Corinthians 12:7-10

42. Psalm 16

43. 1 Corinthians 2:1-5

44. Luke 7:11-17

45. Psalm 103:13-22

FREEDOM FOR LIFE

46. John 8:31-36

47. Galatians 5:16-26

48. Psalm 146

49. 2 Corinthians 3:12-18

50. John 6:63-66

NOTES

INTRODUCTION: A CALL TO SPIRITUAL MATURITY

[1] Kelvin Rodolfo, "What Is Homeostasis?," *Scientific American*, January 3, 2000, www
.scientificamerican.com/article/what-is-homeostasis/.

[2] Elizabeth George, "Starting Your Day with God," Jim & Elizabeth George website,
October 31, 2019, https://elizabethgeorge.com/blogs/devos/starting-your
-day-with-god.

[3] Books I used as resources in the study of Scripture include Frank E. Gaebelein, ed.,
The Expositor's Bible Commentary, vol. 2, with the New International Version
(Zondervan, 1990), 420-27; Molly T. Marshall, *Joining the Dance: A Theology of the
Spirit* (Judson Press, 2003), 185.

1. GOD, I NEED YOUR HELP

[1] John Mark Comer, *The Ruthless Elimination of Hurry* (WaterBrook, 2019), 52.

[2] Aaron Earls, "Scripture Engaged: Who Are American Bible Readers?," Lifeway,
April 27, 2023, https://research.lifeway.com/2023/04/27/scripture-engaged-who
-are-american-bible-readers/.

[3] Earls, "Scripture Engaged: Who Are American Bible Readers?"

[4] Kathleen Cooke, "Why Have Americans Stopped Reading the Bible?" *Christian
Week*, October 16, 2017, www.christianweek.org/americans-stopped-reading
-bible/.

3. STOP. BREATHE. THINK.

[1] Ruth Myers and Warren Myers, *Thirty-One Days of Prayer* (Multnomah, 1997),
Day 1.

[2] "Stop. Breathe. Think," web page, accessed June 12, 2025, www.stopbreathethink
.org.uk.

[3] Parker J. Palmer, *Let Your Life Speak: Listening for the Voice of Vocation* (Jossey-Bass,
2000), 97.

4. BELOVED, COME AWAY

[1] For background on the Jewish Sabbath I referred to Jean-Yves Lacoste, ed., *Encyclo-
pedia of Christian Theology*, vol. 3 (Routledge, 2005), 1405-7.

[2] For background on "breath" and "spirit," I referred to Leland Ryken, James C. Wilhoit,
and Tremper Longman III, eds., *Dictionary of Biblical Imagery* (InterVarsity Press,
1998), 119-20.

[3] Charles Swindoll, "Encouraging Quotes from Pastor Charles Swindoll," *Bible Apolo-
getics—A Daily Devotional* (website), December 30, 2021, https://bible
apologetics.org/encouraging-quotes-from-pastor-charles-swindoll/.

[4] Oswald Chambers, "Do You Walk in White? January 15," *My Utmost for His Highest*,
updated ed. (Discovery House, 1992).

5. TRAINING FOR THE GOLD

[1]David Jeremiah, *Your Daily Journey with God: 365 Daily Devotions* (NavPress, 2011), 123.

[2]Priscilla Shirer, *God Is Able* (B&H, 2013), 42.

7. MEAL TIME: HAVE YOU LOST YOUR APPETITE?

[1]Jeanne Porter King. "'From Superwoman to Well Woman' with Dr. Jeanne Porter King," *Where Ya From* (podcast), episode 75, September 16, 2024, https://youtu.be/9xnjQkd1aak.

8. WELCOME TO THE TABLE

[1]Henri Nouwen, *The Way of the Heart: The Spirituality of the Desert Fathers and Mothers* (HarperOne, 1981), 27.

[2]Doug Petersen, "Beliefs," Ignite America, accessed July 1, 2025, https://ignite america.com/ignite-certifiedstats/.

[3]"Cardinal Spiritual Meaning: What Their Appearance Reveals About Your Life," (blog) Birdfy, accessed July 27, 2025, www.birdfy.com/blogs/blogs/cardinal -spiritual-meaning-what-their-appearance-reveals-about-your-life.

9. THE FAVOR OF GOD

[1]A. W. Tozer, *Knowledge of the Holy: The Attributes of God: Their Meaning in the Christian Life* (HarperSanFrancisco, 1961), 73.

10. SPIRITUAL DIRECTION AND DIVINE PROTECTION

[1]Howard Thurman, "In the Moment of Pause, the Vision of God," *Meditations of the Heart* (Beacon Press, 1981), 29.

[2]Kay Arthur, *Speak to My Heart, God: For Every Need for Every Moment* (Harvest House, 2002), 18.

11. SELF-CARE BEGINS WITH SPIRITUAL INTIMACY

[1]Parker J. Palmer, *Let Your Life Speak: Listening for the Voice of Vocation* (Jossey-Bass, 2000), 49.

12. FUNDAMENTALS FOR QUIET TIMES

[1]J. I. Packer, *Keep in Step with the Spirit: Finding Fullness in Our Walk with God* (Baker Books, 2005), 86.

[2]J. I. Packer, *Knowing God*, 50th anniv. ed. (InterVarsity Press, 1973, 2023), 238.

APPENDIX A: ENERGY ASSESSMENT FOR BALANCE

[1]Energy Assessment for Balance table adapted from Tony Schwartz and Catherine McCarthy, "Manage Your Energy, Not Your Time," *Harvard Business Review*, October 2007, https://hbr.org/2007/10/manage-your-energy-not-your-time. Used with permission of Harvard Business Publishing.

APPENDIX C: SELF-CARE ACTION PLAN

[1]Self-care action plan template adapted from Beyond Boundary Consulting, Hermitage, Tennessee.

Like this book?

Scan the code to discover more content like this!

Get on IVP's email list to receive special offers, exclusive book news, and thoughtful content from your favorite authors on topics you care about.